Cooking Light

pasta
tonight!

Mom & Dad,
We wish you
fun cooking! (Dinner & a cozy
movie
♡ Dave & Erin   together)
Christmas 2016

Cooking Light
pasta
tonight!

Oxmoor House®

ISBN-13: 978-0-8487-3409-1
ISBN-10: 0-8487-3409-2
Library of Congress Control Number: 2009941603

Printed in the United States of America
First Printing 2011

Be sure to check with your health-care provider before making any changes in your diet.

Oxmoor House
VP, Publishing Director: Jim Childs
Editorial Director: Susan Payne Dobbs
Brand Manager: Michelle Turner Aycock
Managing Editor: Laurie S. Herr

Cooking Light® Pasta Tonight!
Senior Editor: Heather Averett
Project Editors: Diane Rose, Holly D. Smith
Senior Designer: Emily Albright Parrish
Director, Test Kitchens: Elizabeth Tyler Austin
Assistant Director, Test Kitchens: Julie Christopher
Test Kitchens Professionals: Allison E. Cox, Julie Gunter,
    Kathleen Royal Phillips, Catherine Crowell Steele,
    Ashley T. Strickland
Photography Director: Jim Bathie
Senior Photo Stylist: Kay E. Clarke
Associate Photo Stylist: Katherine Eckert Coyne
Senior Production Manager: Greg A. Amason

Contributors
Compositor: Diana Morrison
Copy Editor: Dolores Hydock
Indexer: Mary Ann Laurens
Proofreader: Norma Butterworth-McKittrick
Interns: Christine T. Boatwright, Georgia Dodge,
    Allison Sperando, Caitlin Watzke

Cooking Light®
Editor: Scott Mowbray
Creative Director: Carla Frank
Deputy Editor: Phillip Rhodes
Food Editor: Ann Taylor Pittman
Special Publications Editor: Mary Simpson Creel, M.S., R.D.
Nutrition Editor: Kathy Kitchens Downie, R.D.
Associate Food Editors: Timothy Q. Cebula, Julianna Grimes
Associate Editors: Cindy Hatcher, Brandy Rushing
Test Kitchen Director: Vanessa T. Pruett
Assistant Test Kitchen Director: Tiffany Vickers Davis
Chief Food Stylist: Charlotte Autry
Senior Food Stylist: Kellie Gerber Kelley
Recipe Testers and Developers: Robin Bashinsky, Adam Hickman,
    Deb Wise
Art Director: Fernande Bondarenko
Junior Deputy Art Director: Alexander Spacher
Associate Art Director: Rachel Lasserre
Designer: Chase Turberville
Photo Director: Kristen Schaefer
Senior Photographer: Randy Mayor
Senior Photo Stylist: Cindy Barr
Photo Stylist: Leigh Ann Ross
Copy Chief: Maria Parker Hopkins
Assistant Copy Chief: Susan Roberts
Research Editor: Michelle Gibson Daniels
Editorial Production Director: Liz Rhoades
Production Editor: Hazel R. Eddins
Art/Production Assistant: Josh Rutledge
Administrative Coordinator: Carol D. Johnson
CookingLight.com Editor: Allison Long Lowery

To order additional publications, call 1–800–765–6400 or
    1-800-491-0551.

For more books to enrich your life, visit **oxmoorhouse.com**

To search, savor, and share thousands of recipes, visit
myrecipes.com

Cover: Easy Ravioli Bake, page 47
Back cover (clockwise from top left): Alfredo Sauce,
    page 233; Chicken Pasta Soup, page 69; Sausage-Stuffed
    Manicotti, page 41; Braised Short Ribs with Egg Noodles,
    page 133; Salmon, Asparagus, and Orzo Salad with
    Lemon-Dill Vinaigrette, page 81; Colorful Vegetable Lasagna,
    page 175

introduction

Everyone loves pasta! This perennial dinnertime favorite is versatile, straightforward to cook, and in *Cooking Light* recipes, always healthy and delicious. That's why we've pulled from our arsenal of our very best pasta recipes to create *Cooking Light Pasta Tonight!*

This book is brimming with simple, fast, and creative pasta dishes for every type of eater (vegetarians and meat lovers) and every type of occasion (such as casual family suppers to sophisticated special-guest dinners). From fresh-from-the-garden **Pasta Primavera** (page 28) and comforting, meaty **Tomato-Basil Lasagna with Prosciutto** (page 33) to authentic **Italian Sausage Puttanesca** (page 45) and all-American **Creamy Four-Cheese Macaroni** (page 38), this is the ultimate collection of more than 20 years' worth of *Cooking Light* pasta recipes.

But because you want more than just a collection of recipes, we've also included a **Cooking Class**—an all-inclusive guide to all things pasta. It's full of simple how-to photos, techniques, and tips on such topics as making homemade pasta, the pros and cons of dried versus fresh pasta, and mastering the art of al dente, along with glossaries of pasta shapes and international noodles.

With *Cooking Light Pasta Tonight!*, our dedicated staff of culinary professionals and registered dietitians gives you all the tools and recipes you'll need to prepare healthful, delicious pasta dishes any night of the week. Let these kitchen-tested recipes breathe new life into the idea of having *Pasta Tonight!*

The *Cooking Light* Editors

contents

cooking
class

In this Cooking Class, you'll find answers to the most frequently asked questions about pasta and must-have information on selecting, preparing, and serving it—as well as recipes for essential sauces and our top suggestions for using bottled sauces when you're in a pinch. There's no magic required, just loving attention.

Purchasing Pasta

Once pasta is incorporated into a recipe, the different brands all taste about the same, so don't pay more for a fancy name, domestic or imported. What does matter is choosing the right noodle for your dish and cooking it properly.

Dried and Fresh Pasta

Dried pasta is a mixture of water and semolina. In factories, the mix is made into a paste that's turned into different shapes by passing through dies, or large metal discs filled with holes. The pasta is then dried and packaged. When cooked, dried pasta has a nutty wheat flavor and pleasant chewy bite. The *Cooking Light* Test Kitchens mostly use dried pasta in recipes. Fresh pasta is made with regular soft wheat flour, or a combination of other flours, and eggs, giving it a rich flavor and silky texture. It's perishable, so it's generally pricier than dried. Fresh pasta cooks quickly, 2 to 3 minutes on average, making it a handy substitution when you're short on time.

Essential Tips for Cooking Pasta

Cooking pasta is fairly simple, and most packages give directions. Here are some additional recommendations from our staff.

• Put the water on to boil before beginning the rest of the recipe.

• Fill a large pot, such as a Dutch oven or stockpot, with enough water so the pasta can move freely while cooking. (Too little water may cause uneven cooking; too much might overflow.) For 8 ounces of dried pasta, you'll need to use a 4-quart pot.

• Cover the pot, and bring the water to a full rolling boil over high heat.

• It's not necessary to add oil or salt to the cooking water. Sauce won't adhere as well to the pasta's surface when it's cooked with oil. Salt does make pasta taste better on its own, but when it's tossed with a flavorful sauce, there's no need to add extra sodium.

• Add the pasta, and stir with a pasta fork. When the water returns to a rolling boil, start the timer. Stir often. If you use fresh pasta, remember that it cooks more quickly than dried.

• Always cook pasta uncovered over high heat.

• Start testing for doneness a few minutes before the indicated cooking time.

• Set a large colander in the sink so the water drains quickly.

• Do not rinse cooked pasta unless the recipe specifically calls for you to do so. Rinsing washes away some of the starch, making it less sticky. Less starch is ideal for pasta salads that benefit from less stickiness once chilled. But that starch helps the sauce adhere to warm or freshly cooked pasta.

• Return the pasta to the warm cooking pot or add to the skillet with the sauce; toss immediately with large tongs or a pasta fork.

• Pasta can be tricky to serve because it has a tendency to slip and slide. The best serving utensil, especially for longer pasta, is a metal or wooden pasta fork or tongs. For short pasta, a large slotted spoon works fine.

Perfect Pasta

Perfectly cooked pasta has a firm, tender consistency, called "al dente," Italian for "to the tooth." When testing for doneness, remove a piece of pasta from the water, and bite into it. It should offer resistance to the bite but have no trace of brittleness. If an undercooked piece of pasta is cut in half, a white dot or line is clearly visible in the center. Al dente pasta has only a speck of white remaining, meaning the pasta has absorbed just enough water to hydrate it. Cook pasta slightly less than al dente if you're going to cook it for additional time with the sauce.

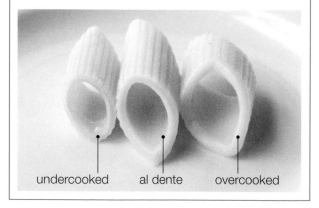

undercooked   al dente   overcooked

Amounts of Dry and Cooked Pasta

Use this guide to help you determine either how much pasta you'll need or how much you'll get. Approximate cooking times are also included.

Type	Dry Measure (8 ounces)	Cooked Volume	Cooking Time
Acini de pepe (small balls similar to orzo)	1¼ cups	3 cups	5 minutes
Alphabets	2 cups	4 cups	5 minutes
Capellini or angel hair	8 ounces	3½ cups	5 minutes
Cavatappi	3 cups	5 cups	8 minutes
Conchiglie rigate (seashell pasta)	3 cups	4 cups	14 minutes
Egg noodles, medium	4 cups	5 cups	5 minutes
Egg noodles, wide	4½ cups	5 cups	5 minutes
Elbow macaroni	2 cups	4 cups	5 minutes
Farfalle (bow tie pasta)	3 cups	4 cups	11 minutes
Fettuccine	8 ounces	4 cups	10 minutes
Fusilli (short twisted spaghetti)	3 cups	4 cups	10 minutes
Gemelli	2 cups	4 cups	10 minutes
Linguine	8 ounces	4 cups	10 minutes
Orecchiette ("little ears" pasta)	2½ cups	4 cups	11 minutes
Orzo (rice-shaped pasta)	1¼ cups	2½ cups	6 minutes
Penne or mostaccioli (tube-shaped pasta)	2 cups	4 cups	10 minutes
Penne rigate	2 cups	4 cups	10 minutes
Perciatelli	8 ounces	4 cups	11 minutes
Radiatore (short coiled pasta)	3 cups	4½ cups	10 minutes
Rigatoni	2½ cups	4 cups	10 minutes
Rotini (corkscrew pasta)	4 cups	4 cups	10 minutes
Small seashell pasta	2 cups	4 cups	8 minutes
Spaghetti	8 ounces	3½ cups	10 minutes
Vermicelli	8 ounces	4 cups	5 minutes
Ziti (short tube-shaped pasta)	3 cups	4 cups	10 minutes

Pasta Shapes

Many varieties of pasta are interchangeable if similar in shape and size (see below). There are also specially shaped pastas, such as lasagna (also available in "no-boil" form) and manicotti, that are used in baked dishes. Ravioli and tortellini are filled with meat, cheese, and other ingredients. Ridged pastas will have "rigati" or "rigate" added to their names.

Long Thin Shapes

- Angel hair
- Fettuccine (small ribbons)
- Linguine
- Spaghetti
- Spaghettini
- Vermicelli

Long Wide Shapes

- Pappardelle

Twisted and Curved Shapes

- Cavatappi
- Elbow macaroni (gomiti)
- Farfalle (bow tie)
- Fusilli (short twisted spaghetti)
- Orecchiette ("little ears")
- Radiatore
- Rotelle (wheels)
- Rotini (corkscrews)
- Seashell macaroni

Tubular Shapes

- Ditalini
- Mezzani
- Mostaccioli
- Penne
- Rigatoni
- Ziti

Pastinas (small pastas)

- Couscous
- Orzo (rice-shaped pasta)
- Pennette
- Tubetti

orecchiette

fusilli

orzo

World of Pasta

Often when we think of pasta, we think of Italian pasta, made from a durum wheat flour, called semolina, and water. Pastas from other cultures, with different tastes, textures, and ingredients, open up a whole new world of possibilities.

Asia

Cellophane noodles: Also called bean threads, these translucent dried noodles are made from the starch of mung beans, potatoes, or green peas.

Chinese egg noodles: Chinese egg noodles are usually made from a dough of wheat flour, eggs, and salt. If they don't contain eggs, they can be labeled "imitation" or "egg-flavored."

Chinese wheat-flour noodles: These noodles are made with flour and water. Many stores offer a wide variety of "flavored" noodles (shrimp, crab, and chicken), and they can be round or flat.

Rice sticks: The most popular of all Asian noodles, rice sticks are made from rice flour and water. Although any type of rice-flour noodle can be called rice sticks, we use this term for flat rice noodles, which are sold mainly in three forms. Thin flat rice noodles most often are used in soups and some stir-fried dishes. Medium-thick rice sticks (called pho in Vietnamese) are all-purpose and can be used in soups, stir-fries, and salads (a slightly wider Thai version is called jantaboon). The widest rice sticks (sha he fen in Chinese) are used in meat, seafood, and vegetable stir-fries.

Soba: Soba noodles from Japan are made with a combination of buckwheat flour, wheat flour, and water. This is one of the few Asian noodles for which there is no substitute.

Somen: The most delicate of noodles, somen are made with wheat flour, a dash of oil, and water. They're served cold with a dipping sauce or hot in soups. The closest substitution would be a very fine pasta, such as capollini or vermicelli.

North Africa

Couscous: Regarded by many as a grain, couscous is actually a pasta made from semolina (durum wheat) flour and salted water. In Tunisia, Algeria, and Morocco, where it's a national favorite, couscous ranges in size from fine- to medium-grained. Another variety, Israeli couscous, is larger.

cellophane noodles

soba noodles

Israeli couscous

Homemade Fettuccine

1¼ cups plus 1 tablespoon all-purpose
   flour, divided
½ teaspoon salt
2 large eggs, lightly beaten

1. Weigh or lightly spoon flour into dry measuring cups; level with a knife. Combine 1 cup flour and salt. Make a well in center of mixture. Add eggs; stir with a fork to gradually incorporate flour into a dough.

2. Turn dough out onto a lightly floured surface; shape into a ball. Knead until smooth and elastic; add enough of remaining flour, 1 tablespoon at a time, to prevent dough from sticking to hands. Wrap in plastic wrap; let rest 10 minutes.

3. Divide dough into 4 equal portions. Working with 1 portion at a time (cover remaining dough with plastic wrap to keep from drying), pass through smooth rollers of pasta machine on widest setting. Continue moving width gauge to narrower settings; pass dough through rollers at each setting, dusting lightly with flour if needed to prevent sticking.

4. Roll dough to about ⅟₁₆ inch. Pass through fettuccine cutting rollers of machine. Hang on a wooden drying rack (dry no longer than 30 minutes). Repeat procedure with remaining dough.

5. Bring 3 quarts water to a rolling boil. Add pasta; cook 2 to 4 minutes or until al dente. Drain; serve immediately. Yield: 6 servings (serving size: ½ cup).

CALORIES 125; FAT 1.9g (sat 0.6g, mono 0.7g, poly 0.3g); PROTEIN 4.9g; CARB 21.2g; FIBER 0.7g; CHOL 71mg; IRON 1.5mg; SODIUM 217mg; CALC 12mg

Essential Techniques for Making Pasta

A simple mixture of flour, salt, and eggs creates a versatile paste that can be shaped, cut, and cooked in a variety of ways. Here, we show you how to make fettuccine. (To make dough in a food processor: Place flour and salt in processor; pulse 3 times or until combined. With processor on, slowly add eggs through food chute; process until dough forms a ball. Follow the essential techniques starting with Step 4.)

Making the Dough

1. Make a well in center of flour mixture, and add eggs.

2. Stir eggs with a fork to gradually incorporate flour and form a dough.

3. Turn dough out onto a lightly floured surface; shape into a ball.

4. Knead until smooth and elastic (about 10 to 15 minutes).

5. Wrap dough in plastic wrap; let rest 10 minutes.

Making the Noodles

6. Pass dough through smooth rollers of pasta machine, beginning on widest setting.

7. Pass dough through cutting rollers of machine.

8. Hang pasta on a wooden drying rack.

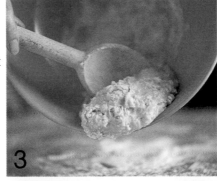

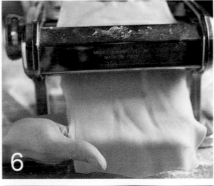

The Essential Sauces

It's almost impossible to think of pasta without thinking of sauce. And though there are some wonderful convenience products on the market (see page 17), sometimes nothing can compare to homemade.

We've included homemade versions of classic Alfredo, arrabbiata, clam, marinara, mushroom, and pesto sauces in the All the Extras chapter (pages 230-243), but here are two more sauces that no pasta lover should be without.

Quick-and-Easy Tomato Sauce

Use this sauce anywhere you might use a store-bought sauce, such as on pasta, in lasagna, or over polenta. Chop the tomatoes in the can with kitchen shears.

    1   tablespoon olive oil
    1½ cups chopped onion
    1   cup chopped green bell pepper
    1   teaspoon dried oregano
    4   garlic cloves, minced
    ½   cup dry red wine
    1   teaspoon dried basil
    ½   teaspoon salt
    ¼   teaspoon black pepper
    2   (28-ounce) cans whole plum tomatoes, undrained and chopped
    1   (6-ounce) can tomato paste
    2   bay leaves

1. Heat oil in a large saucepan over medium-high heat. Add onion, bell pepper, oregano, and garlic; cook 5 minutes or until vegetables are tender, stirring occasionally.
2. Add wine and remaining ingredients, and bring to a boil. Reduce heat, and simmer 30 minutes. Discard bay leaves. Yield: 8 cups (serving size: 1 cup).

CALORIES 93; FAT 2.4g (sat 0.4g, mono 1.4g, poly 0.5g); PROTEIN 3.3g; CARB 17.1g; FIBER 3.3g; CHOL 0mg; IRON 2.4mg; SODIUM 487mg; CALC 77mg

Spaghetti Aglio e Olio

In Italian, aglio e olio (AH-lyoh ay OH-lyoh) means "garlic and oil." Add some crushed red pepper flakes for a spicier version.

    2   tablespoons extra-virgin olive oil
    ¼   teaspoon dried oregano
    4   large garlic cloves, minced
    4   quarts water
    8   ounces uncooked spaghetti
    ½   cup fat-free, lower-sodium chicken broth
    2   tablespoons minced fresh parsley

1. Combine olive oil, oregano, and minced garlic in a small microwave-safe bowl. Cover bowl with wax paper, and microwave at HIGH 1 minute.
2. Bring 4 quarts water to a boil in a large stockpot. Add spaghetti; return to a boil. Cook, uncovered, 10 minutes or until al dente, stirring occasionally. Drain. Return to pot. Stir in garlic mixture and broth. Cook over medium heat 4 minutes or until broth is absorbed, stirring constantly. Stir in parsley. Yield: 4 servings (serving size: 1 cup).

CALORIES 278; FAT 7.7g (sat 1g, mono 5.1g, poly 1g); PROTEIN 7.9g; CARB 43.7g; FIBER 1.5g; CHOL 0mg; IRON 2.4mg; SODIUM 66mg; CALC 20mg

How to Sauce Pasta

When saucing pasta, think of the sauce as a seasoning or dressing that you toss with the pasta, much like a salad and dressing, until each piece of pasta is moist. The idea is to impart well-flavored seasoning to each bite of the finished dish.

Long shapes are generally most compatible with smoother sauces that coat them all over (think of the perfect marriage of fettuccine and Alfredo sauce). Short shapes work well with chunky sauces that can be caught in the nooks and crannies of the pasta.

Store-Bought Pasta Sauce

Supermarket shelves are groaning with jarred pasta sauces. And if you are in a rush, sometimes only a jarred sauce will do. After tasting 11 of them, we concluded that the sauce you pick really does matter. Quality differs tremendously among brands.

Among tomato-basil sauces, we found startling variations in consistency (from watery to pasty) and flavor (from basil-free to far-too-much funny-tasting basil). One sauce tasted like a pot of overcooked onions. But there are very good tomato-basil sauces available, and these are our favorites.

Our Top Pick: Rao's Homemade Tomato Basil Marinara Sauce with Basil

Get it: $9 (24-ounce bottle), available at many large supermarkets and gourmet grocery stores

Testers said: $9 for a jar of tomato sauce? Consider, though: Half a jar can feed four people for a dollar-and-change per diner. Rao's struck tasters as very fresh-tasting, a balanced mix of fruity olive oil, tomato, and basil. This will work in a recipe—such as lasagna—in which you want homemade flavor without the time investment.

Very Good: Bove's Basil Pasta Sauce

Get it: $5 (26-ounce bottle), available at many supermarkets

Testers said: Some raters thought Bove's captured the essence of homemade tomato sauce. It was the only sauce that contained Parmesan cheese, and the cheesy flavor and herby notes gave this sauce a pizzeria quality. Also great for pizzas, calzones, or meatball subs.

Good: Emeril's All Natural Tomato & Basil Pasta Sauce

Get it: $5 (25-ounce bottle), available at supermarkets

Testers said: Most testers noted sweetness and a subtle basil taste. This sauce also received high marks for its tomato flavor and texture, which one rater said was "smooth but not too acidic." Use this sauce in dishes where you can cut its sweetness with fat or spice. Try it in lasagnas or cheese-stuffed shells, in fiery shrimp fra diavolo, or with hot Italian sausage.

Great Value: Classico Tomato & Basil Pasta Sauce

Get it: $3 (24-ounce bottle), available at supermarkets

Testers said: Basil makes a minor appearance in this choice, but many welcomed the garlicky flavor in a slightly thinner tomato-based sauce. Adding a little fresh basil at home yields a balanced option that could work on pizzas or in baked pastas or vegetable soups.

the
classics

Beef Stroganoff

This classic Russian dish is easy to make; use frozen chopped onions and presliced mushrooms to speed preparation. To maintain a creamy consistency, be careful not to bring the sauce to a boil once you stir in the sour cream mixture.

Yield: 8 servings (serving size: ¾ cup beef mixture and 1 cup noodles)

1 (8-ounce) carton reduced-fat sour cream

3 tablespoons no-salt-added tomato paste

1 teaspoon Worcestershire sauce

2.25 ounces all-purpose flour (about ½ cup)

1 teaspoon salt

⅛ teaspoon freshly ground black pepper

2 pounds boneless sirloin steak, cut into 2-inch strips

1 tablespoon butter

½ cup chopped onion

1 (14-ounce) can lower-sodium beef broth

2 cups sliced mushrooms

Chopped fresh parsley (optional)

8 cups cooked medium egg noodles (about 7 cups uncooked pasta)

1. Combine first 3 ingredients in a bowl. Set aside.

2. Weigh or lightly spoon flour into a dry measuring cup; level with a knife. Combine flour, salt, and pepper in a large zip-top plastic bag. Add beef; seal and shake to coat beef with flour mixture.

3. Melt butter in a large nonstick skillet over medium-high heat. Add onion to pan; sauté 2 minutes or until tender. Add beef and flour mixture to pan; sauté 3 minutes or until beef is browned. Gradually add broth, scraping pan to loosen browned bits. Add mushrooms; cover and cook 5 minutes or until mushrooms are tender. Reduce heat to low; gradually stir in sour cream mixture. Cook, uncovered, 1 minute or until heated (do not boil). Stir in parsley, if desired. Serve over egg noodles.

CALORIES 473; FAT 16g (sat 7g, mono 4.3g, poly 1.1g); PROTEIN 30.2g; CARB 50.6g; FIBER 2.6g; CHOL 129mg; IRON 5.7mg; SODIUM 417mg; CALC 81mg

QUICK TIP

The steak will be easier to slice if you partially freeze it first. Slice it diagonally across the grain into thin, 2-inch-long strips.

Angel Hair Pasta with Mussels and Red Pepper Sauce

Sweet red peppers help balance the naturally salty mussels and the slightly acidic tomatoes.

Yield: 4 servings (serving size: 9 mussels, about 1 cup pasta, and about 2 teaspoons parsley)

8 ounces uncooked angel hair pasta

2 teaspoons olive oil

⅓ cup diced onion

1 garlic clove, minced

2 cups diced red bell pepper (about 2 medium)

½ teaspoon salt

Dash of ground red pepper

1 (14.5-ounce) can whole tomatoes, undrained and chopped

½ cup white wine

36 mussels (about 3 pounds), scrubbed and debearded

3 tablespoons chopped fresh parsley

1. Cook pasta according to package directions, omitting salt and fat. Drain; keep warm. Heat oil in a large saucepan over medium-high heat. Add onion and garlic; sauté 5 minutes or until tender. Add bell pepper, salt, and ground red pepper; sauté 2 minutes. Add tomatoes and wine; bring to a boil. Reduce heat to low, and simmer 10 minutes. Add mussels, and increase heat to medium. Cover and simmer 7 minutes or until shells open. Discard any unopened shells. Serve mussel mixture over pasta; sprinkle with parsley.

CALORIES 372; FAT 7.4g (sat 1g, mono 2.6g, poly 1.3g); PROTEIN 24.9g; CARB 46.9g; FIBER 4.5g; CHOL 40mg; IRON 8.7mg; SODIUM 809mg; CALC 85mg

Cavatappi with Tomatoes

The twists, turns, and ridges of cavatappi are perfect for trapping the many flavors of the tomatoes, herbs, cheese, garlic, and breadcrumbs.

Yield: 8 servings (serving size: 1 ramekin)

1 teaspoon chopped fresh thyme

½ teaspoon freshly ground black pepper

2 pints grape tomatoes, halved

Cooking spray

6 quarts of water

2¼ teaspoons salt, divided

1 pound uncooked cavatappi pasta

2 slices applewood-smoked bacon, finely chopped

1 cup finely chopped onion

6 tablespoons all-purpose flour

2 teaspoons minced fresh garlic (about 2 cloves)

4 cups fat-free milk

1½ cups (6 ounces) finely shredded fontina cheese

¾ cup (3 ounces) crumbled blue cheese

¼ cup chopped fresh chives

1½ cups panko (Japanese breadcrumbs)

1 tablespoon butter, melted

1. Preheat oven to 250°.

2. Combine first 3 ingredients on a jelly-roll pan lightly coated with cooking spray. Bake at 250° for 3 hours. Preheat broiler.

3. Bring 6 quarts water to a boil. Add 2 teaspoons salt and pasta; cook 8 minutes or until al dente. Drain.

4. Cook bacon in a saucepan; remove bacon from pan. Add onion to drippings in pan, and cook 4 minutes. Add flour and garlic; cook 1 minute. Stir in 1 cup milk. Gradually add remaining 3 cups milk; bring to a boil. Cook 1 minute, stirring constantly. Remove from heat; let stand 4 minutes. Stir in cheeses. Add remaining ¼ teaspoon salt, bacon, tomatoes, and chives. Add pasta. Divide among 8 (10-ounce) ramekins lightly coated with cooking spray. Combine panko and butter; sprinkle over pasta. Broil 5 minutes.

CALORIES 500; FAT 15.5g (sat 8.4g, mono 4.6g, poly 1.3g); PROTEIN 24.7g; CARB 65.2g; FIBER 3.5g; CHOL 45mg; IRON 3mg; SODIUM 755mg; CALC 328mg

Farfalle with Creamy Wild Mushroom Sauce

This recipe scored high in our Test Kitchens for its rich flavor and ultra-creamy texture. The exotic mushroom blend, a combination of shiitake, cremini, and oyster mushrooms, is sold in eight-ounce packages. If unavailable, you can use all cremini mushrooms.

Yield: 8 servings (serving size: 1¼ cups)

1 pound uncooked farfalle (bow tie pasta)

1 tablespoon butter

12 ounces presliced exotic mushroom blend

½ cup chopped onion

⅓ cup finely chopped shallots

1 tablespoon minced garlic

1½ teaspoons salt, divided

¼ teaspoon freshly ground black pepper

¼ cup dry white wine

⅔ cup whipping cream

½ cup (2 ounces) grated fresh Parmigiano-Reggiano cheese

2 tablespoons chopped fresh parsley

Minced fresh parsley (optional)

1. Cook pasta according to package directions, omitting salt and fat; drain.

2. Melt butter in a large nonstick skillet over medium-high heat. Add mushrooms, onion, shallots, garlic, 1 teaspoon salt, and pepper; cook 12 minutes or until liquid evaporates and mushrooms are tender, stirring occasionally. Add wine; cook 2 minutes or until liquid evaporates, stirring occasionally. Remove from heat.

3. Add cooked pasta, whipping cream, cheese, and 2 tablespoons parsley, tossing gently to coat. Stir in remaining ½ teaspoon salt. Garnish with minced fresh parsley, if desired. Serve immediately.

CALORIES 336; FAT 11.4g (sat 6.9g, mono 3.1g, poly 0.4g); PROTEIN 12.1g; CARB 47.5g; FIBER 2.3g; CHOL 36mg; IRON 2.3mg; SODIUM 577mg; CALC 124mg

INGREDIENT TIP

Bow tie pasta is also known as farfalle pasta. Three cups (or 8 ounces) will yield about 4 cups of cooked pasta. Bow tie pasta on average takes about 11 minutes to cook.

Fettuccine Alfredo

A rich, smooth sauce easily coats the long strands of fettuccine. The two ingredients are a perfect match. Use a spoon to help swirl the noodles neatly onto your fork.

Yield: 6 servings (serving size: 1½ cups)

1 pound uncooked fettuccine

1 tablespoon butter

1¼ cups half-and-half

¾ cup (3 ounces) grated fresh Parmesan cheese

½ teaspoon salt

¼ teaspoon black pepper

1. Cook pasta according to package directions, omitting salt and fat.

2. Melt butter in a large skillet over medium heat. Add half-and-half, cheese, salt, and pepper; cook 1 minute, stirring constantly. Reduce heat; add pasta, tossing gently to coat.

CALORIES 427; FAT 14.6g (sat 7.8g, mono 4.2g, poly 1.3g); PROTEIN 17.2g; CARB 56.5g; FIBER 2.1g; CHOL 105mg; IRON 3.6mg; SODIUM 479mg; CALC 245mg

NUTRITION TIP

We lowered the fat in this classic pasta dish by about 10 grams per serving by using half-and-half instead of whipping cream and decreasing the amount of butter and cheese ever so slightly.

Chicken Marsala

Clarified butter (butter without the milk solids) is ideal for searing meats because it can be heated to a high temperature without burning. Although you can purchase clarified butter, we detail how to make it below in the first step.

Yield: 4 servings (serving size: 1 chicken breast half, 1 cup pasta, and ¼ cup sauce)

4 tablespoons butter, divided

Cooking spray

1 (8-ounce) package presliced mushrooms

2 tablespoons finely chopped shallots

1 tablespoon minced fresh garlic

4 (6-ounce) skinless, boneless chicken breast halves

¼ teaspoon salt, divided

¼ teaspoon black pepper, divided

3 tablespoons all-purpose flour

¾ cup fat-free, lower-sodium chicken broth

½ cup dry Marsala wine

½ cup frozen green peas

2 tablespoons half-and-half

4 cups hot cooked fettuccine (about 8 ounces uncooked pasta)

1. Place 3 tablespoons butter in a small glass measuring cup. Microwave butter at MEDIUM-HIGH 45 seconds or until melted. Let stand 1 minute. Skim foam from surface, and discard (mixture will appear separated). Pour melted butter through a fine sieve over a small bowl, and discard milk solids. Set clarified butter aside.

2. Heat a large nonstick skillet over medium-high heat. Coat pan with cooking spray. Add mushrooms, shallots, and garlic to pan. Cook 3 minutes or until moisture evaporates; remove mushroom mixture from pan. Set aside.

3. Place each chicken breast half between 2 sheets of heavy-duty plastic wrap; pound to ¼-inch thick using a meat mallet or small heavy skillet. Sprinkle both sides of chicken with ⅛ teaspoon salt and ⅛ teaspoon pepper. Place flour in a shallow dish; dredge chicken breast halves in flour.

4. Add clarified butter to pan, and place over medium-high heat. Add chicken; cook 3 minutes on each side or until lightly browned. Remove chicken from pan. Return mushroom mixture to pan; add broth and Marsala, scraping pan to loosen browned bits.

5. Bring mixture to a boil, reduce heat, and simmer 5 minutes or until reduced to 1 cup. Stir in peas; cook 1 minute. Add remaining 1 tablespoon butter, half-and-half, remaining ⅛ teaspoon salt, and remaining ⅛ teaspoon pepper, stirring until butter melts. Return chicken to pan; cook until thoroughly heated. Serve chicken and sauce over pasta.

CALORIES 585; FAT 15.3g (sat 8.4g, mono 4.1g, poly 1g); PROTEIN 51.4g; CARB 55g; FIBER 3.7g; CHOL 133mg; IRON 4.4mg; SODIUM 469mg; CALC 57mg

Pasta Primavera

Fresh and flavorful, this pasta primavera chock full of vegetables makes a lovely entrée for spring. A combination of equal parts milk and cream, half-and-half creates a silky, full-bodied sauce.

Yield: 4 servings (serving size: 2 cups pasta mixture, 1 tablespoon basil, and 1 tablespoon cheese)

2 cups green beans, trimmed and halved crosswise

2 cups broccoli florets

½ cup (1-inch) slices asparagus (about 2 ounces)

6 ounces uncooked fettuccine

1 tablespoon olive oil

1 cup chopped onion

2 teaspoons minced fresh garlic

⅛ teaspoon crushed red pepper

½ cup fresh or frozen green peas

1 cup grape tomatoes, halved

⅔ cup half-and-half

1 teaspoon cornstarch

¾ teaspoon salt

¼ cup chopped fresh basil

¼ cup (1 ounce) shaved Parmigiano-Reggiano cheese

1. Cook green beans in boiling water 1 minute. Add broccoli and asparagus; cook 2 minutes or until vegetables are crisp-tender. Remove vegetables from pan with a slotted spoon; place in a large bowl. Return water to a boil. Add pasta; cook 10 minutes or until al dente. Drain and add to vegetable mixture.
2. Heat oil in a large nonstick skillet over medium-high heat. Add 1 cup onion, and sauté 2 minutes. Add garlic and red pepper; sauté 3 minutes or until onion begins to brown.
3. Add peas, and sauté 1 minute. Add tomatoes; sauté 2 minutes. Combine half-and-half and cornstarch, stirring with a whisk. Reduce heat to medium. Add half-and-half mixture and salt to pan; cook 1 minute or until sauce thickens, stirring constantly. Pour sauce over pasta mixture; toss gently to coat. Sprinkle with basil and cheese. Serve immediately.

CALORIES 338; FAT 10.8g (sat 4.7g, mono 4.4g, poly 0.8g); PROTEIN 13.7g; CARB 49.6g; FIBER 7.1g; CHOL 20mg; IRON 2.9mg; SODIUM 607mg; CALC 205mg

WINE NOTE

Because this is a cream-based pasta primavera, consider serving it with a pinot blanc.

Ragù alla Bolognese with Fettuccine

Ragùs are rich and flavorful meat sauces that begin with a soffrito—minced aromatic vegetables sautéed in oil. Wine is often added and reduced. Ragùs are typical rustic fare in neighborhood trattorias in Italy. This recipe is adapted from the classic ragùs of Italy's Emilia-Romagna region.

Yield: 8 servings (serving size: 1½ cups)

1 tablespoon olive oil

1. Heat oil in a large Dutch oven over medium heat. Add onion, celery, and carrot; cover and cook 8 minutes, stirring occasionally. Remove onion mixture from pan.

2. Add veal, pork, and beef to pan; cook over medium heat until browned, stirring to crumble. Add wine, salt, pepper, nutmeg, and bay leaf; bring to a boil. Cook 5 minutes. Add onion mixture, broth, and tomato puree; bring to a simmer. Cook 1 hour, stirring occasionally.

3. Stir in milk and minced parsley; bring to a boil. Reduce heat, and simmer 40 minutes.

4. Discard bay leaf. Add pasta, and toss to coat. Sprinkle evenly with cheese. Garnish with parsley sprigs, if desired.

CALORIES 369; FAT 11.8g (sat 4.2g, mono 4.8g, poly 1.4g); PROTEIN 21.4g; CARB 44g; FIBER 4.2g; CHOL 87mg; IRON 3.7mg; SODIUM 546mg; CALC 117mg

WINE NOTE

The best all-around choice when a recipe calls for dry white wine is a quality American sauvignon blanc. Wine contributes flavors to the final dish, so don't be tempted to use anything of a lesser caliber.

Tomato-Basil Lasagna with Prosciutto

Dish this up at your next supper club or family get-together, and you'll have everyone raving and going back for more. Serve with a big tossed salad and some garlic bread to round out the meal.

Yield: 9 servings

5 garlic cloves

1 (16-ounce) carton 1% low-fat cottage cheese

½ cup (4 ounces) block-style fat-free cream cheese

¼ cup (1 ounce) grated fresh Romano cheese, divided

2½ teaspoons dried basil

½ teaspoon crushed red pepper

1 large egg

1 (26-ounce) bottle fat-free tomato-basil pasta sauce (such as Muir Glen)

Cooking spray

12 cooked lasagna noodles

1 cup (4 ounces) chopped prosciutto or ham

1 cup (4 ounces) shredded part-skim mozzarella cheese

1. Preheat oven to 375°.

2. Drop garlic through food chute with food processor on, and process until minced. Add cottage cheese; process 2 minutes or until smooth. Add cream cheese, 2 tablespoons Romano, basil, pepper, and egg; process until well blended.

3. Spread ½ cup pasta sauce in bottom of a 13 x 9–inch baking dish coated with cooking spray. Arrange 3 noodles over pasta sauce; top with 1 cup cheese mixture, ⅓ cup prosciutto, and ¾ cup pasta sauce. Repeat layers twice, ending with noodles. Spread remaining pasta sauce over noodles. Sprinkle with remaining 2 tablespoons Romano and mozzarella.

4. Cover and bake at 375° for 45 minutes or until sauce is bubbly. Uncover and bake an additional 15 minutes. Let lasagna stand 5 minutes.

CALORIES 272; FAT 5.6g (sat 2.8g, mono 1.8g, poly 0.6g); PROTEIN 20.8g; CARB 33g; FIBER 2.1g; CHOL 47mg; IRON 2.3mg; SODIUM 775mg; CALC 213mg

MAKE AHEAD TIP

After assembling the lasagna, cover and freeze it for up to one month. When ready to serve, thaw in refrigerator and then bake as directed.

Chicken Parmesan

You can prepare the pasta sauce in advance; refrigerate or freeze in an airtight container. Cook the linguine while the chicken bakes.

Yield: 4 servings (serving size: 1 chicken breast half, ¾ cup pasta sauce, ¼ cup cheese, and ½ cup linguine)

1.1 ounces all-purpose flour (about ¼ cup)

¼ cup grated Parmesan cheese

¼ teaspoon black pepper

4 (6-ounce) skinless, boneless chicken breast halves

1 large egg white, lightly beaten

1 tablespoon olive oil

Cooking spray

3 cups Quick-and-Easy Tomato Sauce

1 cup (4 ounces) shredded part-skim mozzarella cheese

4 ounces uncooked linguine

Fresh basil sprigs (optional)

1. Preheat oven to 350°.
2. Weigh or lightly spoon flour into a dry measuring cup; level with a knife. Combine flour, Parmesan cheese, and ¼ teaspoon pepper in a shallow dish.
3. Place each chicken breast half between 2 sheets of heavy-duty plastic wrap; pound to ¼-inch thick using a meat mallet or small heavy skillet. Dip each chicken breast half in egg white; dredge in flour mixture.
4. Heat oil in a large nonstick skillet over medium-high heat. Add chicken, and cook 5 minutes on each side until golden. Arrange chicken in a 13 x 9–inch baking dish coated with cooking spray. Pour Quick-and-Easy Tomato Sauce over chicken. Sprinkle with mozzarella. Bake at 350° for 15 minutes.
5. Cook linguine according to package directions, omitting salt and fat. Drain. Serve chicken and sauce over linguine. Garnish with fresh basil sprigs, if desired.

CALORIES 506; FAT 15.4g (sat 6.1g, mono 6.6g, poly 1.5g); PROTEIN 43.4g; CARB 48.6g; FIBER 5.9g; CHOL 90mg; IRON 3.5mg; SODIUM 634mg; CALC 340mg

Quick-and-Easy Tomato Sauce

Yield: 3 cups (serving size ¾ cup)

1 teaspoon olive oil

1 cup chopped onion

4 garlic cloves, minced

½ cup dry red wine or 2 tablespoons balsamic vinegar

1 tablespoon sugar

1 tablespoon chopped fresh basil or 2 teaspoons dried basil

2 tablespoons tomato paste

½ teaspoon dried Italian seasoning

¼ teaspoon black pepper

2 (14.5-ounce) cans diced tomatoes, undrained

2 tablespoons chopped fresh parsley

1. Heat oil in a saucepan or large skillet over medium-high heat. Add onion and garlic; sauté 5 minutes. Stir in wine and next 6 ingredients, and bring to a boil. Reduce heat to medium, and cook, uncovered, about 15 minutes. Stir in parsley.

CALORIES 96; FAT 1.3g (sat 0.2g, mono 0.9g, poly 0.2g); PROTEIN 2.9g; CARB 20.6g; FIBER 4.7g; CHOL 0mg; IRON 1.3mg; SODIUM 331mg; CALC 57mg

Linguine with Clam Sauce

Because this dish is so fresh and simple, you will absolutely want to use fresh clams. Use the larger amount of red pepper for a zestier dish.

Yield: 6 servings (serving size: 1⅓ cups pasta mixture and 6 clams)

¼ cup olive oil, divided

2 garlic cloves, minced

⅓ cup clam juice

¼ cup chopped fresh flat-leaf parsley

½ to ¾ teaspoon crushed red pepper

½ teaspoon salt

¼ teaspoon freshly ground black pepper

3 dozen littleneck clams

8 cups hot cooked linguine (about 1 pound uncooked pasta)

1. Heat 2 tablespoons oil in a large skillet over medium heat. Add garlic; cook 3 minutes or until golden, stirring frequently. Stir in clam juice and next 5 ingredients. Cover and cook 10 minutes or until clams open. Discard any unopened shells.

2. Place pasta in a large bowl. Add remaining 2 tablespoons oil; toss well to coat. Add clam mixture to pasta; toss well.

CALORIES 398; FAT 10.6g (sat 1.6g, mono 6.7g, poly 0.9g); PROTEIN 17.4g; CARB 58.4g; FIBER 2.6g; CHOL 19mg; IRON 10.3mg; SODIUM 258mg; CALC 46mg

INGREDIENT TIP

Cleaning clams is quick and easy. Scrub them with a stiff brush under cold running water to remove sand and dirt.

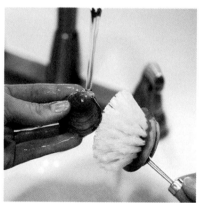

Creamy Four-Cheese Macaroni

The combination of fontina, Parmesan, cheddar, and processed cheese packs a flavor punch. Fresh Parmesan and a good extrasharp cheddar are essential.

Yield: 8 servings (serving size: 1 cup)

1.5 ounces all-purpose flour (about ⅓ cup)

2⅔ cups 1% low-fat milk

¾ cup (3 ounces) shredded fontina cheese or Swiss cheese

½ cup (2 ounces) grated fresh Parmesan cheese

½ cup (2 ounces) shredded extrasharp cheddar cheese

3 ounces light processed cheese, cubed (such as Kraft Velveeta 2% Milk)

6 cups cooked elbow macaroni (about 3 cups uncooked)

¼ teaspoon salt

Cooking spray

⅓ cup crushed onion Melba toasts (about 12 pieces)

1 tablespoon reduced-calorie butter, softened

1. Preheat oven to 375°.

2. Weigh or lightly spoon flour into a dry measuring cup, and level with a knife. Place flour in a large saucepan. Gradually add milk, stirring with a whisk until blended. Cook over medium heat 8 minutes or until thick, stirring constantly. Add cheeses; cook 3 minutes or until cheeses melt, stirring frequently. Remove from heat; stir in macaroni and salt.

3. Spoon mixture into a 2-quart casserole coated with cooking spray. Combine crushed toasts and butter in a small bowl; stir until well blended. Sprinkle over macaroni mixture. Bake at 375° for 30 minutes or until bubbly.

CALORIES 350; FAT 11.2g (sat 6.3g, mono 2.9g, poly 0.9g); PROTEIN 18g; CARB 42.4g; FIBER 2.1g; CHOL 32mg; IRON 1.9mg; SODIUM 497mg; CALC 306mg

FLAVOR TIP

Often found on top of soups and salads or as an accompaniment to dips and spreads,

Melba toast adds flavor without adding many calories or fat. The crispiness of the toasts is a wonderful contrast to the creamy cheese and tender noodles.

Beef, Cheese, and Noodle Bake

This family-friendly casserole is a great way to incorporate more vegetables into your kids' food. For creamiest results, do not overbake.

Yield: 8 servings (serving size: about 1 cup)

1 (8-ounce) package small elbow macaroni

Cooking spray

1 cup prechopped onion

1 cup preshredded carrot

2 teaspoons bottled minced garlic

1 pound lean ground sirloin

1 cup tomato sauce

1 teaspoon kosher salt, divided

½ teaspoon freshly ground black pepper

1 cup fat-free milk

2 tablespoons all-purpose flour

⅛ teaspoon ground nutmeg

1½ cups (6 ounces) reduced-fat shredded sharp cheddar cheese (such as Cracker Barrel), divided

1. Preheat oven to 350°.

2. Cook pasta according to package directions, omitting salt and fat; drain. Lightly coat pasta with cooking spray.

3. Heat a Dutch oven over medium-high heat. Coat pan with cooking spray. Add onion and carrot, and sauté 4 minutes. Add garlic; sauté 1 minute. Add beef; cook 5 minutes or until browned, stirring to crumble. Add tomato sauce, ½ teaspoon salt, and pepper. Cook 2 minutes or until most of liquid evaporates.

4. Add pasta to beef mixture in pan, stirring to combine. Spoon pasta mixture into an 11 x 7–inch baking dish coated with cooking spray.

5. Place milk, flour, nutmeg, and remaining ½ teaspoon salt in a medium saucepan; stir with a whisk until blended. Cook over medium heat 2 minutes or until thick, stirring constantly with a whisk. Add 1 cup cheese, stirring until smooth. Pour cheese mixture over pasta mixture; stir. Top evenly with remaining ½ cup cheese. Bake at 350° for 20 minutes or until lightly browned. Let stand 5 minutes before serving.

CALORIES 283; FAT 7.7g (sat 4.2g, mono 2.4g, poly 0.7g); PROTEIN 22.3g; CARB 30.1g; FIBER 2.1g; CHOL 46mg; IRON 3.1mg; SODIUM 622mg; CALC 209mg

NUTRITION TIP

With more than 200 milligrams of calcium per serving, this dish is a good source of the bone-building mineral.

Sausage-Stuffed Manicotti

Like most baked pastas, this dish requires a good bit of time to prepare, but we believe you'll discover it's definitely worth the extra effort.

Yield: 10 servings (serving size: 1 stuffed manicotti)

10 uncooked manicotti

Cooking spray

1 pound sweet turkey Italian sausage

1½ cups chopped onion

1 cup chopped green bell pepper

2 tablespoons butter

2 tablespoons all-purpose flour

2 cups fat-free milk

⅛ teaspoon black pepper

1½ cups (6 ounces) shredded part-skim mozzarella cheese

2 cups tomato-basil pasta sauce (such as Newman's Own)

¼ cup (1 ounce) grated fresh Parmesan cheese

1. Cook pasta according to package directions, omitting salt and fat.

2. Heat a large nonstick skillet over medium-high heat. Coat pan with cooking spray. Remove casings from sausage. Add sausage to pan; cook 5 minutes or until browned, stirring to crumble. Add onion and bell pepper to pan; sauté 5 minutes or until tender.

3. Melt butter in a medium saucepan over medium heat. Stir in flour; cook 2 minutes, stirring constantly with a whisk. Remove from heat; gradually add milk, stirring with a whisk. Return pan to heat; bring to a boil. Cook 6 minutes or until thick, stirring constantly with a whisk. Remove from heat; stir in black pepper. Add ½ cup milk mixture to sausage mixture; stir well.

4. Preheat oven to 350°.

5. Spoon about ⅓ cup sausage mixture into each manicotti; arrange manicotti in a single layer in a 13 x 9–inch baking dish coated with cooking spray. Sprinkle mozzarella over manicotti; spread remaining milk mixture evenly over mozzarella. Top milk mixture with pasta sauce, spreading to cover. Sprinkle with Parmesan. Bake at 350° for 35 minutes or until bubbly.

CALORIES 292; FAT 11.5g (sat 4.9g, mono 3.5g, poly 1.8g); PROTEIN 19.6g; CARB 25.8g; FIBER 1.4g; CHOL 57mg; IRON 1.8mg; SODIUM 719mg; CALC 193mg

Mediterranean Orzo Salad with Feta Vinaigrette

Make a colorful dinner salad inspired by the Mediterranean in less than 30 minutes. Use part of the artichoke marinade in the vinaigrette to boost flavor and save time.

Yield: 4 servings (serving size: 1¼ cups salad and about 1 tablespoon cheese)

1 cup uncooked orzo (rice-shaped pasta; about 8 ounces)

2 cups bagged prewashed baby spinach, chopped

½ cup chopped drained oil-packed sun-dried tomato halves

3 tablespoons chopped red onion

3 tablespoons chopped pitted kalamata olives

½ teaspoon freshly ground black pepper

¼ teaspoon salt

1 (6-ounce) jar marinated artichoke hearts, undrained

¾ cup (3 ounces) feta cheese, crumbled and divided

1. Cook orzo according to package directions, omitting salt and fat. Drain; rinse with cold water. Combine orzo, spinach, and next 5 ingredients in a large bowl.

2. Drain artichokes, reserving marinade. Coarsely chop artichokes, and add artichokes, reserved marinade, and ½ cup feta cheese to orzo mixture, tossing gently to coat. Sprinkle each serving with remaining feta cheese.

CALORIES 338; FAT 11g (sat 3.8g, mono 2.7g, poly 0.5g); PROTEIN 11.9g; CARB 52g; FIBER 5.1g; CHOL 19mg; IRON 3mg; SODIUM 620mg; CALC 138mg

EQUIPMENT TIP

An easy-to-use pitter is the perfect tool to handily remove olive and cherry pits when you are making quick and easy weeknight dishes.

Italian Sausage Puttanesca

Puttanesca (poot-tah-NEHS-kah) sauce is a spicy mélange of tomatoes, onions, capers, olives, anchovies, and garlic. Add mixed greens and fresh bread to complete the meal.

Yield: 6 servings

8 ounces uncooked penne

Cooking spray

8 ounces hot turkey Italian sausage

1 cup chopped onion

1 cup chopped green bell pepper

3 garlic cloves, minced

½ cup halved pitted kalamata olives

2 tablespoons tomato paste

1 tablespoon capers, drained

1 teaspoon anchovy paste

2 (14.5-ounce) cans no-salt-added whole tomatoes, undrained and chopped

½ cup (2 ounces) finely shredded Parmesan cheese

1. Preheat oven to 400°.

2. Cook pasta according to package directions, omitting salt and fat. Drain well.

3. Heat a Dutch oven over medium-high heat. Coat pan with cooking spray. Remove casings from sausage. Add sausage, onion, bell pepper, and garlic to pan; sauté 8 minutes, stirring to crumble sausage.

4. Add olives, tomato paste, capers, anchovy paste, and tomatoes to pan; bring to a boil. Reduce heat, and simmer 5 minutes. Remove from heat. Add pasta, tossing well to combine. Spoon pasta mixture into an 11 x 7–inch baking dish coated with cooking spray; sprinkle evenly with cheese. Bake at 400° for 15 minutes or until cheese melts and begins to brown.

CALORIES 321; FAT 10.6g (sat 3.1g, mono 4.6g, poly 1.6g); PROTEIN 14.8g; CARB 41.8g; FIBER 4g; CHOL 28mg; IRON 3.1mg; SODIUM 649mg; CALC 152mg

FLAVOR TIP

For a little less heat, use sweet turkey Italian sausage instead of hot.

Easy Ravioli Bake

This recipe pairs the convenience of store-bought pasta with a quick, easy, homemade sauce. Use any variety of ravioli.

Yield: 6 servings

2 (9-ounce) packages refrigerated chicken ravioli (such as Monterey Pasta Company)

Cooking spray

1 cup chopped onion

½ cup chopped green bell pepper

½ teaspoon dried oregano

4 garlic cloves, minced

¼ cup dry white wine

½ teaspoon dried basil

¾ teaspoon salt

¼ teaspoon crushed red pepper

⅛ teaspoon black pepper

4 (14.5-ounce) cans no-salt-added whole tomatoes, undrained and chopped

6 tablespoons tomato paste

½ cup (2 ounces) shredded part-skim mozzarella cheese

1. Cook pasta according to package directions, omitting salt and fat. Drain well.
2. Preheat oven to 400°.
3. Heat a Dutch oven over medium-high heat. Coat pan with cooking spray. Add onion, bell pepper, oregano, and garlic; sauté 5 minutes or until vegetables are tender. Add wine and next 6 ingredients, stirring well to combine; bring to a boil. Reduce heat, and simmer 20 minutes, stirring often. Remove from heat. Add pasta to tomato mixture, tossing well to combine. Spoon pasta mixture into a 13 x 9–inch baking dish lightly coated with cooking spray; sprinkle evenly with cheese. Bake at 400° for 30 minutes or until cheese melts and begins to brown.

CALORIES 330; FAT 8.1g (sat 4.8g, mono 2g, poly 0.7g); PROTEIN 16.3g; CARB 49.8g; FIBER 5g; CHOL 46mg; IRON 3.6mg; SODIUM 715mg; CALC 167mg

QUICK TIP

Chopping whole tomatoes in the can is a quick and easy way to speed up meal preparation.

Simply snip them with kitchen scissors, and you're done. No mess to clean up.

Two-Pepper Rigatoni and Cheese

While this is a great, basic recipe on its own, it also offers possibilities for variations with different pastas and cheeses.

Yield: 8 servings (serving size: 1 cup)

5 cups uncooked rigatoni
(16 ounces uncooked pasta)

2 tablespoons butter, divided

1 cup chopped red bell pepper

3 tablespoons all-purpose flour

3 cups fat-free milk

1 cup (4 ounces) shredded fontina cheese

1 cup (4 ounces) shredded sharp cheddar cheese

1 tablespoon finely chopped pickled jalapeño pepper

¾ teaspoon salt

½ cup sliced green onions

Cooking spray

2 (1-ounce) slices white bread

1. Preheat oven to 375°.

2. Cook pasta according to package directions, omitting salt and fat. Drain well; place in a large bowl.

3. Melt 1 tablespoon butter in a large saucepan over medium-high heat. Add bell pepper; sauté 5 minutes or until tender. Add to pasta.

4. Add flour to pan. Gradually add milk, stirring with a whisk until smooth. Bring to a boil; cook 2 minutes or until thick, stirring constantly. Remove from heat. Add cheeses, stirring until cheeses melt and mixture is smooth. Stir in jalapeño and salt. Add cheese mixture to pasta, tossing well to coat. Stir in green onions. Spoon pasta mixture into a 13 x 9–inch baking dish coated with cooking spray.

5. Place bread slices in a food processor; pulse 10 times or until coarse crumbs measure about 1 cup. Melt remaining 1 tablespoon butter. Combine butter and breadcrumbs in a small bowl; toss until blended. Sprinkle breadcrumb mixture over pasta mixture. Bake at 375° for 15 minutes or until browned.

CALORIES 408; FAT 12.8g (sat 7.8g, mono 3.3g, poly 0.6g); PROTEIN 19.2g; CARB 54.5g; FIBER 2.4g; CHOL 40mg; IRON 2.5mg; SODIUM 550mg; CALC 293mg

Marinara Sauce over Rotini

If you don't have rotini, try another pasta—just about any pasta will do, even spaghetti.
Top with Parmesan cheese for an extra-special treat.

Yield: 4 servings (serving size: 1 cup pasta and ¾ cup sauce)

1 teaspoon olive oil

½ cup chopped onion

2 garlic cloves, minced

2 tablespoons chopped fresh or
2 teaspoons dried basil

2 tablespoons chopped fresh or
2 teaspoons dried parsley

1 teaspoon sugar

½ teaspoon dried oregano

¼ teaspoon salt

¼ teaspoon black pepper

1 (28-ounce) can diced tomatoes,
undrained

1 tablespoon capers

4 cups hot cooked rotini (about 4
cups uncooked corkscrew pasta)

1. Heat oil in a medium saucepan over medium heat. Add onion and garlic, and sauté 2 minutes. Add basil and next 6 ingredients; bring to a boil.
2. Reduce heat, and simmer 15 minutes, stirring occasionally. Stir in capers. Serve over pasta.

CALORIES 277; FAT 2.5g (sat 0.4g, mono 1g, poly 0.7g); PROTEIN 9.7g; CARB 54.7g; FIBER 3.3g; CHOL 0mg; IRON 3.7mg; SODIUM 531mg; CALC 77mg

QUICK TIP

If you don't have any fresh herbs or garlic on hand and don't have time to swing by the supermarket, dried herbs and bottled minced garlic make good stand-ins.

Four-Cheese Stuffed Shells with Smoky Marinara

Yield: 2 casseroles, 5 servings per dish (serving size: about 4 stuffed shells and about ½ cup Smoky Marinara)

1 pound uncooked jumbo shell pasta (40 shells)

Cooking spray

1 (12-ounce) carton 1% low-fat cottage cheese

1 (15-ounce) carton ricotta cheese

1 cup (4 ounces) shredded Asiago cheese

¾ cup (3 ounces) grated fresh Parmesan cheese

2 tablespoons chopped fresh chives

2 tablespoons chopped fresh parsley

¼ teaspoon black pepper

¼ teaspoon salt

1 (10-ounce) package frozen chopped spinach, thawed, drained, and squeezed dry

6 cups Smoky Marinara, divided

1 cup (4 ounces) shredded part-skim mozzarella cheese, divided

1. Cook pasta according to package directions, omitting salt and fat. Drain and set aside.
2. Preheat oven to 375°.
3. Coat 2 (13 x 9–inch) baking dishes with cooking spray; set aside.
4. Place cottage cheese and ricotta cheese in a food processor; process until smooth. Combine cottage cheese mixture, Asiago, and next 6 ingredients.
5. Spoon or pipe 1 tablespoon cheese mixture into each shell. Arrange half of stuffed shells, seam sides up, in 1 prepared dish. Pour 3 cups Smoky Marinara over stuffed shells. Sprinkle with ½ cup mozzarella. Repeat procedure with remaining stuffed shells, Smoky Marinara, and mozzarella in remaining prepared dish.
6. Cover with foil. Bake at 375° for 30 minutes or until thoroughly heated.

CALORIES 470; FAT 15.7g (sat 8.8g, mono 4.7g, poly 0.9g); PROTEIN 28.3g; CARB 52.7g; FIBER 5.3g; CHOL 47mg; IRON 3.8mg; SODIUM 916mg; CALC 508mg

Smoky Marinara

Yield: 6 cups (serving size: ½ cup)

1 tablespoon olive oil

3 garlic cloves, minced

¼ cup chopped fresh basil

2 tablespoons chopped fresh parsley

2 tablespoons chopped fresh oregano

2 teaspoons balsamic vinegar

⅛ teaspoon salt

⅛ teaspoon pepper

1 (28-ounce) can crushed fire-roasted tomatoes, undrained

1 (28-ounce) can crushed tomatoes, undrained

1. Heat oil in a large saucepan over medium heat. Add garlic, basil, parsley, and oregano; sauté 1 minute, stirring frequently. Stir in vinegar and remaining ingredients. Reduce heat, and simmer 10 minutes.

CALORIES 55; FAT 1.2g (sat 0.2g, mono 0.8g, poly 0.1g); PROTEIN 2.3g; CARB 9g; FIBER 2.3g; CHOL 0mg; IRON 0.9mg; SODIUM 350mg; CALC 49mg

Spaghetti and Meatballs

Yield: 8 servings (serving size: 1 cup spaghetti, about ½ cup sauce, 4 meatballs, and 1 tablespoon cheese)

Sauce:

Cooking spray

1 cup finely chopped onion

3 garlic cloves, minced

2 tablespoons tomato paste

¼ teaspoon salt

1 (14-ounce) can lower-sodium beef broth

2 (28-ounce) cans whole peeled tomatoes, undrained and chopped

Meatballs:

1 (1-ounce) slice white bread

2 (4-ounce) links sweet turkey Italian sausage, casings removed

½ cup finely chopped onion

⅓ cup chopped fresh basil

¼ cup chopped fresh flat-leaf parsley

2 tablespoons egg substitute

½ teaspoon freshly ground black pepper

¼ teaspoon salt

2 garlic cloves, minced

1 large egg

1 pound ground sirloin

Remaining Ingredients:

½ cup chopped fresh flat-leaf parsley

⅓ cup chopped fresh basil

1 pound hot cooked spaghetti

½ cup (2 ounces) grated fresh Parmigiano-Reggiano cheese

Flat-leaf parsley sprigs (optional)

1. To prepare sauce, heat a large nonstick skillet over medium-high heat. Coat pan with cooking spray. Add 1 cup onion; sauté 3 minutes. Add garlic, and sauté 1 minute. Add tomato paste; cook 1 minute. Stir in ¼ teaspoon salt and broth; cook 4 minutes. Stir in tomatoes. Reduce heat, and simmer 45 minutes, stirring occasionally.

2. Preheat broiler.

3. To prepare meatballs, place bread in a food processor, and process until fine crumbs measure ½ cup. Combine breadcrumbs, sausage, ½ cup onion, and next 8 ingredients in a bowl. With wet hands, shape meat mixture into 32 meatballs. Place meatballs on a broiler pan. Broil 15 minutes or until done. Add meatballs to sauce; simmer 15 minutes. Sprinkle with ½ cup parsley and ⅓ cup basil. Serve over spaghetti. Sprinkle with cheese; garnish with parsley sprigs, if desired.

CALORIES 291; FAT 8g (sat 3.2g, mono 2.5g, poly 1.3g); PROTEIN 24.3g; CARB 32.2g; FIBER 4.1g; CHOL 76mg; IRON 7.4mg; SODIUM 873mg; CALC 163mg

Spaghetti Carbonara

For a simple, tasty supper, you can't go wrong with this recipe. And if you have leftover ham, it's even better because chopped ham replaces the bacon in this version of the classic Italian dish.

Yield: 4 servings (serving size: 1 cup)

8 ounces uncooked spaghetti

1 cup chopped cooked ham

⅓ cup (1½ ounces) grated Parmigiano-Reggiano or Parmesan cheese

¼ cup reduced-fat sour cream

½ teaspoon salt

2 large eggs, lightly beaten

1 garlic clove, minced

¼ teaspoon coarsely ground black pepper

1. Cook pasta according to package directions, omitting salt and fat. Drain pasta in a colander over a bowl, reserving ½ cup liquid.

2. Heat a large nonstick skillet over medium heat. Add ham, and cook 2 minutes or until thoroughly heated. Add pasta, and stir well. Combine cheese and next 4 ingredients, stirring with a whisk. Add reserved pasta liquid to egg mixture, stirring with a whisk. Pour egg mixture over pasta mixture; stir well. Cook over low heat 5 minutes or until sauce thickens, stirring constantly (do not boil). Sprinkle with pepper.

CALORIES 352; FAT 9.6g (sat 4.6g, mono 2.2g, poly 0.9g); PROTEIN 21g; CARB 45g; FIBER 1.4g; CHOL 139mg; IRON 1.7mg; SODIUM 748mg; CALC 179mg

SAFETY TIP

We updated this recipe by lightly beating the eggs, and then combining them with the cheese and sour cream. This allows the mixture to cook over low heat, ensuring that the eggs are cooked thoroughly.

Spaghettini with Oil and Garlic

In Italian, simple garlic and olive oil sauce is known as aglio e olio. This classic pasta dish comes together quickly, so it's a good weeknight dinner. Just pair it with a green salad and a bottle of wine. Spaghettini is in between the sizes of vermicelli and spaghetti, so either of those is a good substitute. Be careful not to overcook the garlic because browned garlic tastes bitter. Push the garlic to one side of the pan so it will cook evenly.

Yield: 8 servings

6 quarts water

2¾ teaspoons salt, divided

1 pound uncooked spaghettini

2 tablespoons extra-virgin olive oil

10 garlic cloves, sliced

½ cup chopped fresh flat-leaf parsley

½ teaspoon crushed red pepper

1 cup (4 ounces) grated Parmigiano-Reggiano cheese

1. Bring 6 quarts water and 2 teaspoons salt to a boil in a large stockpot. Stir in pasta; partially cover, and return to a boil, stirring frequently. Cook 6 minutes or until pasta is almost al dente, stirring occasionally. Drain pasta in a colander over a bowl, reserving 1 cup cooking water.

2. While pasta cooks, heat oil in a large nonstick skillet over medium heat. Add garlic; cook 2 minutes or until fragrant or beginning to turn golden, stirring constantly. Remove from heat; stir in remaining ¾ teaspoon salt, reserved 1 cup cooking water, parsley, and pepper.

3. Add pasta to pan, stirring well to coat. Return pan to medium heat; cook 1 minute or until pasta is al dente, tossing to coat. Place 1 cup pasta mixture in each of 8 bowls; sprinkle each serving with 2 tablespoons cheese. Serve immediately.

CALORIES 303; FAT 8g (sat 2.9g, mono 3.7g, poly 0.8g); PROTEIN 12.7g; CARB 44.4g; FIBER 1.6g; CHOL 10mg; IRON 2.6mg, SODIUM 603mg; CALC 190mg

Turkey Tetrazzini

Many believe this dish was named after the opera singer Luisa Tetrazzini. This easy version has all the rich taste of traditional tetrazzini but takes less time to prepare. Serve with fresh green beans.

Yield: 6 servings (serving size: about 1⅔ cups)

10 ounces uncooked vermicelli

2 teaspoons vegetable oil

1 pound turkey breast cutlets

¾ teaspoon onion powder, divided

½ teaspoon salt, divided

¼ teaspoon black pepper, divided

2 tablespoons dry sherry

2 (8-ounce) packages presliced mushrooms

¾ cup frozen green peas, thawed

¾ cup fat-free milk

⅔ cup fat-free sour cream

⅓ cup (about 1½ ounces) grated fresh Parmesan cheese

1 (10¾-ounce) can reduced-fat cream of chicken soup (such as Healthy Choice)

Cooking spray

⅓ cup dry breadcrumbs

2 tablespoons butter, melted

1. Preheat oven to 450°.
2. Cook pasta according to package directions, omitting salt and fat. Drain.
3. Heat oil in a large nonstick skillet over medium-high heat. Sprinkle turkey with ½ teaspoon onion powder, ¼ teaspoon salt, and ⅛ teaspoon pepper. Add turkey to pan; cook 2 minutes on each side or desired degree of doneness. Remove turkey from pan.
4. Add remaining ¼ teaspoon onion powder, sherry, and sliced mushrooms to pan. Cover and cook 4 minutes or until mushrooms are tender.
5. Combine peas, milk, sour cream, cheese, and soup in a large bowl. Chop turkey. Add remaining ¼ teaspoon salt, remaining ⅛ teaspoon pepper, pasta, turkey, and mushroom mixture to soup mixture, tossing gently to combine. Spoon mixture into a 13 x 9–inch baking dish coated with cooking spray.
6. Combine breadcrumbs and butter in a small dish, tossing to combine. Sprinkle breadcrumb mixture over pasta mixture. Bake at 450° for 12 minutes or until bubbly and thoroughly heated.

CALORIES 459; FAT 14.8g (sat 5.9g, mono 4.4g, poly 2.8g); PROTEIN 30.5g; CARB 48.1g; FIBER 3.1g; CHOL 69mg; IRON 4mg; SODIUM 716mg; CALC 199mg

MAKE AHEAD TIP

This is a great recipe to make ahead and refrigerate; bake it just before you're ready to serve it.

soups
& salads

Turkey-Pasta Soup

To cook the pasta properly, make sure the soup is boiling when you add the ditali and that it comes back to a boil for the rest of the cooking time.

Yield: 8 servings (serving size: 1½ cups)

1 tablespoon olive oil

½ cup chopped carrot

¼ cup chopped celery

¼ cup minced onion

1 garlic clove, minced

2 cups water

⅓ cup chopped 33%-lower-sodium ham (about 2 ounces)

¼ teaspoon freshly ground black pepper

4 (14-ounce) cans fat-free, lower-sodium chicken broth

1 cup uncooked ditali (about 4 ounces short tube-shaped macaroni)

3 cups chopped cooked turkey

3 cups thinly sliced napa (Chinese) cabbage

1. Heat oil in a large Dutch oven over medium-high heat. Add carrot, celery, onion, and garlic; sauté 3 minutes or until tender. Add 2 cups water, ham, pepper, and broth; bring to a boil.

2. Add pasta; cook 8 minutes or until pasta is done. Stir in turkey and cabbage; cook 2 minutes or until cabbage wilts.

CALORIES 194; FAT 4.9g (sat 1.3g, mono 2g, poly 1g); PROTEIN 21.8g; CARB 14.2g; FIBER 1.2g; CHOL 44mg; IRON 1.6mg; SODIUM 483mg; CALC 45mg

Chicken, Pasta, and Chickpea Stew

To make the soup ahead, omit the pasta and refrigerate or freeze the soup. As the soup reheats over medium heat, cook pasta separately according to package directions, and then stir shortly before serving. Use leaves from celery stalks as a garnish.

Yield: 6 servings (serving size: about 1½ cups soup and 1 tablespoon cheese)

Cooking spray

1 cup thinly sliced celery

¾ cup diced carrot

½ cup chopped onion

2 garlic cloves, minced

4 cups fat-free, lower-sodium chicken broth

3 cups Basic Marinara (recipe on page 239)

1 cup canned chickpeas (garbanzo beans), rinsed and drained

¾ cup uncooked ditalini (very short tube-shaped macaroni)

½ teaspoon freshly ground black pepper

8 ounces skinless, boneless chicken thighs, cut into ½-inch pieces

6 tablespoons shaved fresh Parmesan cheese

1. Heat a Dutch oven over medium heat. Coat pan with cooking spray. Add celery, carrot, and onion to pan; cook 12 minutes or until tender, stirring occasionally. Add garlic; cook 30 seconds, stirring constantly. Add broth and next 4 ingredients; bring to a boil. Reduce heat, and simmer 12 minutes or until pasta is tender. Add chicken to pan; cook 3 minutes or until chicken is done. Sprinkle with cheese.

CALORIES 237; FAT 7.1g (sat 2g, mono 3.2g, poly 1.5g); PROTEIN 15.5g; CARB 28.1g; FIBER 5.8g; CHOL 29mg; IRON 2.5mg; SODIUM 724mg; CALC 138mg

Red Bean Stew with Ditalini

This hearty stew is a one-dish meal in the truest sense. Add the uncooked ditalini straight to the pot—it cooks right along with the stew.

Yield: 4 servings (serving size: 1½ cups stew and 1 tablespoon cheese)

1 tablespoon olive oil

1½ cups presliced mushrooms

1 cup diced carrot

1½ cups water

¼ teaspoon black pepper

1 (15-ounce) can kidney beans, rinsed and drained

1 (14.5-ounce) can diced tomatoes, undrained

1 (14-ounce) can lower-sodium beef broth

4 ounces uncooked ditalini (very short tube-shaped macaroni)

2 tablespoons commercial pesto (such as Alessi)

¼ cup (1 ounce) shredded fresh Parmesan cheese

1. Heat oil in a Dutch oven over medium-high heat. Add mushrooms and carrot; sauté 4 minutes. Stir in 1½ cups water and next 4 ingredients. Cover; bring to a boil. Stir in pasta; cook, uncovered, 11 minutes or until pasta is done. Stir in pesto; sprinkle each serving with cheese.

CALORIES 324; FAT 10.2g (sat 2.3g, mono 4.7g, poly 1.7g); PROTEIN 15.2g; CARB 43.7g; FIBER 10.4g; CHOL 6mg; IRON 3.1mg; SODIUM 560mg; CALC 150mg

INGREDIENT TIP

Made of garlic, basil, pine nuts, Parmesan or Romano cheese, and olive oil, pesto can be

spread onto toasted bread, used in place of red sauce on pizzas, or blended into a soup or stew, as it is in this recipe.

Lemon Chicken Orzo Soup

Chicken noodle soup is probably the top comfort food of all time. You'll need to start a day ahead to prepare the tasty homemade broth.

Yield: 8 servings (serving size: about 1¾ cups)

1 (4-pound) whole chicken

2 carrots, peeled, cut into 1-inch pieces

2 celery stalks, cut into 1-inch pieces

1 medium onion, peeled and sliced

6 garlic cloves, crushed

4 sprigs fresh flat-leaf parsley

2 teaspoons whole black peppercorns

2 bay leaves

6 cups water

1⅓ cups chopped carrot

1¼ cups chopped onion

1 cup chopped celery

2 teaspoons salt

8 ounces uncooked orzo (rice-shaped pasta)

¼ cup chopped fresh flat-leaf parsley

2½ teaspoons grated lemon rind

¼ cup fresh lemon juice

Lemon wedges (optional)

Coarsely cracked black pepper (optional)

1. Remove and discard giblets and neck from chicken. Place chicken in a large Dutch oven. Add 2 chopped carrots, 2 chopped celery stalks, and next 5 ingredients to pan. Add 6 cups water; bring to a simmer. Reduce heat, and simmer 45 minutes.

2. Remove chicken from pan; place chicken in a bowl. Chill 15 minutes. Discard skin; remove chicken from bones, discarding bones. Chop chicken into bite-sized pieces; cover and chill. Strain broth mixture through a sieve into a large bowl; discard solids. Cool broth mixture to room temperature. Cover and chill 8 to 24 hours. Skim fat from surface; discard.

3. Add enough water to broth to equal 9 cups; place broth mixture in a large Dutch oven. Add 1⅓ cups carrot, 1¼ cups onion, 1 cup celery, and salt to pan; bring to a boil. Cover, reduce heat, and simmer 15 minutes or until vegetables are tender. Add reserved chicken, and simmer 3 minutes or until thoroughly heated. Keep warm.

4. Cook pasta according to package directions, omitting salt and fat. Add pasta to pan with chicken and broth mixture; stir in parsley, rind, and juice. Garnish each serving with lemon wedges and cracked black pepper, if desired.

CALORIES 235; FAT 5.2g (sat 1.3g, mono 1.8g, poly 1.1g); PROTEIN 21.3g; CARB 24.6g; FIBER 2.3g; CHOL 53mg; IRON 1.1mg; SODIUM 679mg; CALC 39mg

Chicken Pasta Soup

This quick twist on classic chicken noodle soup is loaded with fresh vegetables—carrots, celery, onion, and green bell pepper. You'll agree 100 percent that fresh is best.

Yield: 6 servings (serving size: 1½ cups)

Cooking spray

2 (6-ounce) skinless, boneless chicken breasts, cut into bite-sized pieces

1 (8-ounce) container refrigerated prechopped celery, onion, and bell pepper mix

1 cup matchstick-cut carrots

¼ teaspoon freshly ground black pepper

7 cups fat-free, lower-sodium chicken broth

1 cup uncooked whole-wheat rotini (corkscrew pasta)

1. Heat a Dutch oven over medium-high heat. Coat pan with cooking spray.

2. Add chicken and next 3 ingredients; cook 6 minutes or until chicken begins to brown and vegetables are tender, stirring frequently. Add broth; bring to a boil. Add pasta, reduce heat to medium, and cook 8 minutes or until pasta is done.

CALORIES 156; FAT 3g (sat 0.6g, mono 0.6g, poly 0.4g); PROTEIN 20.4g; CARB 12.8g; FIBER 2.8g; CHOL 40mg; IRON 1.4mg; SODIUM 723mg; CALC 27mg

Pasta e Fagioli

Here's a comforting soup that's ready in less than 30 minutes. Hot turkey sausage, mellow cannellini beans, and tender seashell pasta combine to create a speedy weeknight dinner.

Yield: 6 servings (serving size: 1 cup)

1 tablespoon olive oil

6 ounces hot turkey Italian sausage

1½ tablespoons bottled minced garlic

1 cup water

1 (14-ounce) can fat-free, lower-sodium chicken broth

1 (8-ounce) can no-salt-added tomato sauce

1 cup uncooked small seashell pasta (about 4 ounces)

½ cup grated Romano cheese, divided

1½ teaspoons dried oregano

¼ teaspoon salt

¼ teaspoon white pepper

2 (15-ounce) cans cannellini beans or other white beans, rinsed and drained

Minced fresh parsley (optional)

Crushed red pepper (optional)

1. Heat oil in a large saucepan over medium-high heat. Add sausage and garlic; sauté 2 minutes or until browned, stirring to crumble. Add water, broth, and tomato sauce; bring to a boil. Stir in pasta, ¼ cup cheese, oregano, salt, pepper, and beans; bring to a boil. Cover, reduce heat, and simmer 8 minutes or until pasta is done. Let stand 5 minutes; sprinkle with remaining ¼ cup cheese. Garnish each serving with parsley and red pepper, if desired.

CALORIES 353; FAT 10.2g (sat 3.1g, mono 4.1g, poly 2.3g); PROTEIN 20.5g; CARB 45.6g; FIBER 4.5g; CHOL 34mg; IRON 4.5mg; SODIUM 742mg; CALC 177mg

QUICK TIP

Canned cannellini beans are a good choice for this soup because they're more convenient than

soaking dried beans and hold their shape well during the short cook time.

Sun-Dried Tomato–Tortellini Soup

Fix it in a flash—this filling soup comes together in about 20 minutes. And it tastes even better the next day.

Yield: 6 servings (serving size: about 1½ cups)

1½ teaspoons olive oil

1 cup chopped onion

1 cup (¼-inch-thick) slices carrot

⅔ cup chopped celery

2 garlic cloves, minced

5 cups fat-free, lower-sodium chicken broth

2 cups water

1¼ cups sun-dried tomato halves, packed without oil, chopped (about 3 ounces)

½ teaspoon dried basil

¼ teaspoon freshly ground black pepper

1 bay leaf

3 cups (about 12 ounces) fresh cheese tortellini

1 cup chopped bok choy

1. Heat oil in a large Dutch oven over medium-high heat. Add onion, carrot, celery, and garlic; sauté 5 minutes. Add broth and next 5 ingredients; bring to a boil. Reduce heat; simmer 2 minutes. Add pasta and bok choy, and simmer 7 minutes or until pasta is done. Discard bay leaf.

CALORIES 256; FAT 8g (sat 2.6g, mono 3.9g, poly 0.7g); PROTEIN 12.1g; CARB 33.9g; FIBER 3.9g; CHOL 25mg; IRON 1.1mg; SODIUM 681mg; CALC 47mg

INGREDIENT TIP

Whether packed in oil or dry-packed, sun-dried tomatoes add vivid flavor and a healthy dose of lycopene to your cooking. To make chopping dry-packed tomatoes easier, coat a chef's knife with cooking spray; it will keep the tomatoes from sticking to the blade.

Cheese Tortellini and Vegetable Soup

This hearty soup is reminiscent of the Italian classic minestrone. Though minestrone traditionally uses macaroni, we've substituted fresh cheese tortellini for better flavor and to speed preparation. Serve with a tossed spinach salad to round out the meal.

Yield: 6 servings (serving size: 1⅓ cups)

1 (14.5-ounce) can diced tomatoes with garlic and onion, undrained

1 (11½-ounce) can condensed bean with bacon soup (such as Campbell's), undiluted

3 cups water

1 (16-ounce) package frozen Italian-style vegetables

¾ teaspoon dried Italian seasoning

¼ teaspoon freshly ground black pepper

½ (9-ounce) package fresh cheese tortellini

¼ cup grated Parmesan cheese

1. Combine first 6 ingredients in a 4-quart saucepan; cover and bring to a boil over high heat. Add pasta; reduce heat to medium. Cook, partially covered, 7 minutes or until pasta and vegetables are tender. Stir in cheese.

CALORIES 201; FAT 4g (sat 1.4g, mono 0.7g, poly 0.3g); PROTEIN 10.3g; CARB 31.3g; FIBER 5.4g; CHOL 11mg; IRON 2.1mg; SODIUM 920mg; CALC 66mg

Udon Soup with Shrimp

Although homemade dashi (Japanese seaweed broth) is part of the easy beauty of this dish, you can substitute instant dashi in a pinch. If you take that shortcut, infuse the broth with fresh ginger.

Yield: 4 servings

2 large sheets kombu (kelp)

2 quarts cold water

1 cup bonito flakes (about ¼ ounce)

1 (1-inch) piece fresh ginger, peeled and thinly sliced

1 ounce dried mushroom blend

1 (14-ounce) package fresh jumbo udon noodles

2 green onions, trimmed

1 tablespoon sugar

2½ tablespoons lower-sodium soy sauce

2 tablespoons rice vinegar

1 pound medium shrimp, peeled and deveined

1. Wipe kombu clean with a cloth; cut sheeting lengthwise into 3-inch pieces. Place kombu in a large saucepan over medium-high heat; cover with 2 quarts cold water. Heat mixture to 180° or until tiny bubbles form around edge (do not boil). Reduce heat to medium-low, and simmer 20 minutes. Remove from heat; discard kombu. Stir in bonito and ginger; let stand 10 minutes or until bonito sinks. Strain through a cheesecloth-lined colander over a bowl; discard solids.

2. Wipe pan clean. Return broth to pan; bring to a boil. Remove from heat. Stir in mushrooms; let stand 20 minutes. Strain mixture through a cheesecloth-lined colander over a bowl, reserving mushrooms and broth. Wipe pan clean. Return broth to pan; bring to a simmer. Coarsely chop mushrooms.

3. Cook noodles according to package directions; drain. Cut onions into 1-inch pieces; cut each piece in half lengthwise. Cut onion pieces lengthwise into thin strips. Combine sugar, soy sauce, and vinegar in a small bowl, stirring well. Add shrimp to broth; cook 1 minute. Stir in mushrooms; cook 30 seconds. Remove from heat; stir in vinegar mixture. Place about 1 cup noodles in each of 4 bowls; top with 2 cups broth mixture. Divide onion strips evenly among bowls.

CALORIES 429; FAT 3g (sat 0.5g, mono 0.4g, poly 1.2g); PROTEIN 28.9g; CARB 65.5g; FIBER 2.2g; CHOL 147mg; IRON 4.3mg; SODIUM 994mg; CALC 74mg

Peppery Monterey Jack Pasta Salad

Acini di pepe (ah-CHEE-nee dee PAY-pay) are tiny pasta rounds resembling peppercorns. Use ditalini (very short tube-shaped macaroni) or any other small pasta shape if you can't find acini di pepe in your supermarket. Serve with Asiago breadsticks.

Yield: 4 servings (serving size: about 1½ cups)

6 ounces uncooked acini di pepe pasta (about 1 cup)

2¼ cups diced plum tomato (about 14 ounces)

⅓ cup capers, rinsed and drained

¼ cup finely chopped red onion

¼ cup sliced pickled banana pepper

¼ cup chopped fresh parsley

2 tablespoons cider vinegar

1 tablespoon extra-virgin olive oil

½ teaspoon dried oregano

⅛ teaspoon salt

2 ounces Monterey Jack cheese, cut into ¼-inch cubes

1 (16-ounce) can navy beans, rinsed and drained

1 ounce salami, chopped

1 garlic clove, minced

1. Cook pasta according to package directions, omitting salt and fat. Drain.

2. Combine tomato and next 12 ingredients in a large bowl. Add pasta to tomato mixture, tossing well to combine.

CALORIES 371; FAT 11.6g (sat 4.7g, mono 5.3g, poly 1.4g); PROTEIN 16.6g; CARB 51.7g; FIBER 6.3g; CHOL 21mg; IRON 3.5mg; SODIUM 919mg; CALC 164mg

Asian Pasta Salad

Use any combination of nuts and seeds. This salad would also be good with sliced bell pepper or shiitake mushrooms. Serve as an accompaniment to pepper steak or pork chops glazed with hoisin sauce. Look for plain wheat noodles for this salad.

Yield: 12 servings (serving size: about ¾ cup)

2 tablespoons sliced almonds

2 tablespoons unsalted sunflower seed kernels

1 (8-ounce) package Chinese noodles, crumbled (such as KA-ME)

⅓ cup white wine vinegar

⅓ cup lower-sodium beef broth

¼ cup sugar

2 tablespoons canola oil

¼ teaspoon salt

¼ teaspoon freshly ground black pepper

1 cup chopped green onions

1 (10-ounce) package angel hair slaw

1. Heat a medium nonstick skillet over medium heat. Add almonds, sunflower seed kernels, and noodles to pan; cook 3 minutes or until lightly toasted, stirring frequently.

2. Combine vinegar, broth, sugar, oil, salt, and pepper in a small bowl, stirring with a whisk.

3. Combine toasted noodle mixture, green onions, and slaw in a large bowl. Add vinegar mixture, tossing well to combine. Let stand 5 minutes before serving.

CALORIES 130; FAT 4g (sat 0.3g, mono 1.9g, poly 1.3g); PROTEIN 3g; CARB 20.9g; FIBER 1.5g; CHOL 0mg; IRON 0.5mg; SODIUM 165mg; CALC 12mg

Couscous-Chickpea Salad with Ginger-Lime Dressing

Turmeric lends a golden hue to the pasta, but it can be omitted.

Yield: 6 servings (serving size: 1⅓ cups)

Dressing:

⅓ cup fresh lime juice

1½ tablespoons extra-virgin olive oil

2 teaspoons grated peeled fresh ginger

¾ teaspoon ground cumin

½ teaspoon sugar

½ teaspoon salt

¼ teaspoon freshly ground black pepper

1 garlic clove, minced

Salad:

2 cups water

1½ cups uncooked couscous

½ cup raisins

½ teaspoon ground turmeric

1 cup chopped tomato

1 cup chopped peeled cucumber

1 cup (4 ounces) crumbled feta cheese

¼ cup thinly sliced green onions

2 tablespoons finely chopped fresh mint

1 (15½-ounce) can chickpeas (garbanzo beans), rinsed and drained

1. To prepare dressing, combine first 8 ingredients, stirring with a whisk.

2. To prepare salad, bring 2 cups water to a boil in a medium saucepan, and gradually stir in couscous, raisins, and turmeric. Remove from heat; cover and let stand 5 minutes. Fluff with a fork. Place couscous mixture in a large bowl. Add tomato and next 5 ingredients. Drizzle with dressing; stir well to coat. Cover and chill at least 1 hour.

CALORIES 345; FAT 9g (sat 3.4g, mono 3.8g, poly 1.2g); PROTEIN 11.2g; CARB 56.2g; FIBER 5.6g; CHOL 17mg; IRON 2mg; SODIUM 529mg; CALC 137mg

MAKE AHEAD TIP

Couscous is great for make-ahead salads like this one. It's extremely versatile and cooks quickly. And for this recipe, it's even better when chilled.

Salmon, Asparagus, and Orzo Salad with Lemon-Dill Vinaigrette

This savory salad is quick, easy, and loaded with flavorful ingredients such as crisp-tender asparagus, perfectly cooked pink salmon, red onion, and a refreshing lemon juice–based vinaigrette. It received our highest Test Kitchen rating.

Yield: 6 servings (serving size: about 1¼ cups)

6 cups water

1 pound asparagus, trimmed and cut into 3-inch pieces

1 cup uncooked orzo (rice-shaped pasta)

1 (1¼-pound) skinless salmon fillet

¼ teaspoon salt

¼ teaspoon freshly ground black pepper

Cooking spray

¼ cup thinly sliced red onion

⅓ cup Lemon-Dill Vinaigrette

1. Preheat broiler.

2. Bring 6 cups water to a boil in a large saucepan. Add asparagus; cook 3 minutes or until crisp-tender. Remove asparagus from water with tongs or a slotted spoon, reserving water in pan. Plunge asparagus into ice water; drain and set aside.

3. Return reserved water to a boil. Add orzo, and cook according to package directions, omitting salt and fat.

4. While orzo cooks, sprinkle fillet evenly with salt and pepper. Place fish on a foil-lined broiler pan coated with cooking spray. Broil 5 minutes or until desired degree of doneness. Using 2 forks, break fish into large chunks. Combine fish, orzo, asparagus, onion, and Lemon-Dill Vinaigrette in a large bowl; toss gently to coat.

CALORIES 310; FAT 11g (sat 3.2g, mono 4.7g, poly 2g); PROTEIN 26g; CARB 24.6g; FIBER 2.2g; CHOL 56mg; IRON 1.4mg; SODIUM 333mg; CALC 67mg

Lemon-Dill Vinaigrette

Yield: ⅓ cup (serving size: about 1 tablespoon)

⅓ cup (1.3 ounces) crumbled feta cheese

1 tablespoon chopped fresh dill

3 tablespoons fresh lemon juice

2 teaspoons extra-virgin olive oil

¼ teaspoon salt

¼ teaspoon freshly ground black pepper

1. Combine all ingredients in a small bowl, stirring well with a whisk.

CALORIES 43; FAT 4g (sat 1.7g, mono 1.8g, poly 0.2g); PROTEIN 1.4g; CARB 1.2g; FIBER 0.1g; CHOL 8mg; IRON 0.1mg; SODIUM 214mg; CALC 48mg

Easy Penne and Tuna Salad

Instead of cleaning out the fridge to put dinner together, toss pasta with quality tuna; its richness and flavor will carry the salad, which is embellished with simple flavorings. Serve with a torn baguette.

Yield: 4 servings (serving size: 2 cups)

1 large red bell pepper

4 quarts water

2¼ teaspoons salt, divided

6 ounces uncooked penne pasta

2 cups coarsely chopped arugula

¼ cup thinly sliced shallots

2 tablespoons red wine vinegar

1 tablespoon capers, drained

1 tablespoon extra-virgin olive oil

1 (7.8-ounce) jar premium tuna packed in oil (such as Ortiz), drained and flaked

Freshly ground black pepper (optional)

1. Preheat broiler.

2. Cut bell pepper in half lengthwise; discard seeds and membranes. Place pepper halves, skin sides up, on a foil-lined baking sheet; flatten with hand. Broil 15 minutes or until blackened. Place in a zip-top plastic bag; seal. Let stand 15 minutes. Peel and chop.

3. Bring 4 quarts water and 2 teaspoons salt to a boil in a large saucepan. Cook pasta according to package directions, omitting additional salt and fat. Drain and rinse with cold water; drain well.

4. Combine bell pepper, pasta, remaining ¼ teaspoon salt, arugula, and remaining ingredients in a large bowl; toss well. Garnish with freshly ground black pepper, if desired.

CALORIES 310; FAT 8.8g (sat 1.4g, mono 4.3g, poly 2.3g); PROTEIN 21.4g; CARB 36.3g; FIBER 2.5g; CHOL 17mg; IRON 2.2mg; SODIUM 556mg; CALC 34mg

Tex-Mex Pasta Salad

This kid-friendly recipe is a takeoff on macaroni and cheese; it makes a large batch that holds well for two or three days. Serve with pickled jalapeño slices for grownups who like spicy food.

Yield: 12 servings (serving size: about 1⅓ cups)

1 pound uncooked radiatore (short coiled pasta)

2 teaspoons olive oil

3 garlic cloves, minced

1½ pounds ground turkey

⅔ cup water

1 (1.25-ounce) package 40%-less-sodium taco seasoning (such as Old El Paso)

2 cups (8 ounces) preshredded reduced-fat Mexican blend cheese

2 cups chopped seeded tomato

1 cup chopped bell pepper

½ cup chopped fresh cilantro

½ cup chopped green onions

½ cup sliced ripe olives

1 (15.5-ounce) can black beans, rinsed and drained

2 tablespoons fresh lime juice

½ teaspoon salt

¼ teaspoon ground cumin

1 (8-ounce) container reduced-fat sour cream

Salsa (optional)

1. Cook pasta according to package directions, omitting salt and fat. Drain and rinse with cold water. Drain; set aside.

2. Heat oil in a large nonstick skillet over medium-high heat. Add garlic; sauté 1 minute.

3. Add turkey; cook until browned, stirring to crumble. Stir in ⅔ cup water and taco seasoning; bring to a boil. Reduce heat, and simmer 4 minutes or until liquid almost evaporates and turkey is done, stirring frequently. Remove from heat; cool slightly.

4. Combine pasta, turkey mixture, reduced-fat cheese, and next 6 ingredients in a large bowl.

5. Combine lime juice, salt, cumin, and sour cream, stirring until well blended. Pour over pasta mixture; toss gently to coat. Serve with salsa, if desired.

CALORIES 344; FAT 11.4g (sat 5.3g, mono 4.1g, poly 1.4g); PROTEIN 23.4g; CARB 38.5g; FIBER 3.6g; CHOL 51mg; IRON 2.9mg; SODIUM 632mg; CALC 193mg

NUTRITION TIP

Rinsing canned beans gets rid of the thick liquid in the can and reduces the sodium by 40 percent.

Thai Noodle Salad with Sautéed Tofu

This colorful salad is a zesty one-dish meal. Leftovers are great chilled or at room temperature. For a pronounced nutty flavor, use roasted peanut oil.

Yield: 6 servings (serving size: about 2 cups)

Tofu:

¾ pound firm water-packed tofu, drained

2 tablespoons fresh lime juice

1 tablespoon lower-sodium soy sauce

1 tablespoon chili garlic sauce (such as Lee Kum Kee)

1 teaspoon sugar

2 teaspoons grated peeled fresh ginger

½ teaspoon crushed red pepper

2 garlic cloves, minced

1 tablespoon peanut oil

Noodles:

¾ pound uncooked rice vermicelli

Dressing:

¼ cup fresh lime juice

3 tablespoons chili garlic sauce

2 tablespoons lower-sodium soy sauce

2 tablespoons peanut oil

1 tablespoon Thai fish sauce (such as Three Crabs)

2 teaspoons sugar

2 teaspoons grated peeled fresh ginger

¼ teaspoon salt

¼ teaspoon crushed red pepper

Remaining Ingredients:

2 cups thinly sliced romaine lettuce

1 cup shredded carrot

½ cup chopped fresh cilantro

¼ teaspoon salt

1. To prepare tofu, cut tofu into ¾-inch-thick slices. Arrange tofu slices in a single layer on several layers of paper towels. Top with several more layers of paper towels; top with a cast-iron skillet or other heavy pan. Let stand 30 minutes. Remove tofu from paper towels; cut into ¾-inch cubes. Combine tofu, 2 tablespoons juice, and next 6 ingredients in a zip-top plastic bag. Seal and marinate at room temperature 2 hours, turning bag occasionally.

2. Heat a large nonstick skillet over medium-high heat. Add 1 tablespoon oil to pan, swirling to coat; heat 30 seconds. Remove tofu from bag; discard marinade. Add tofu to pan; sauté 5 minutes or until crisp, carefully turning to brown all sides. Remove from heat.

3. To prepare noodles, while tofu marinates, place vermicelli in a large bowl. Cover with boiling water. Let stand 20 minutes or until tender. Drain and rinse under cold water; drain well. Set noodles aside.

4. To prepare dressing, combine ¼ cup juice and next 8 ingredients, stirring with a whisk.

5. Combine vermicelli, lettuce, and next 3 ingredients in a large bowl. Add dressing; toss well to combine. Top with tofu.

CALORIES 336; FAT 9.8g (sat 1.5g, mono 5g, poly 2.8g); PROTEIN 10.3g; CARB 57.2g; FIBER 2.4g; CHOL 0mg; IRON 2.5mg; SODIUM 794mg; CALC 132mg

INGREDIENT TIP

Draining tofu under a weight expels moisture, making the sautéed tofu crisp.

Chicken, Bean, and Blue Cheese Pasta Salad with Sun-Dried Tomato Vinaigrette

You can substitute asparagus for the green beans, but be sure to cook the asparagus spears only 1 to 2 minutes or until crisp-tender.

Yield: 4 servings (serving size: 1 cup)

1½ cups uncooked rotini (corkscrew pasta)

1½ cups (2-inch) cut green beans (about 6 ounces)

2 cups diced cooked chicken breast (about ¾ pound)

¼ cup (1 ounce) crumbled blue cheese

¼ cup Sun-Dried Tomato Vinaigrette

1. Cook pasta according to package directions, omitting salt and fat. Add beans during last 5 minutes of cooking. Drain pasta and beans; rinse with cold water until cool.

2. Combine pasta mixture and remaining ingredients; toss gently to coat.

CALORIES 315; FAT 9g (sat 2.7g, mono 3.9g, poly 1.1g); PROTEIN 28.8g; CARB 30.1g; FIBER 2.8g; CHOL 65mg; IRON 2.5mg; SODIUM 192mg; CALC 75mg

Sun-Dried Tomato Vinaigrette

Yield: ¼ cup (serving size: 1 tablespoon)

2 tablespoons balsamic vinegar

1 tablespoon olive oil

1 tablespoon water

2 tablespoons chopped sun-dried tomatoes, packed without oil

1 tablespoon chopped fresh basil

1 tablespoon chopped red onion

1. Combine first 3 ingredients in a small bowl, stirring well with a whisk. Stir in tomatoes, basil, and onion.

CALORIES 43; FAT 4g (sat 0.5g, mono 2.5g, poly 0.5g); PROTEIN 0.3g; CARB 2.6g; FIBER 0.3g; CHOL 0mg; IRON 0.2mg; SODIUM 37mg; CALC 6mg

Seashell Salad with Buttermilk-Chive Dressing

While this creamy salad is delicious when served immediately, it is equally good the next day. The flavors meld beautifully overnight.

Yield: 4 servings (serving size: about 1¼ cups salad and 1 tablespoon prosciutto)

8 ounces uncooked seashell pasta

1 cup frozen green peas

¼ cup organic canola mayonnaise

¼ cup fat-free buttermilk

1 tablespoon minced fresh chives

1 teaspoon chopped fresh thyme

½ teaspoon salt

½ teaspoon freshly ground black pepper

2 garlic cloves, minced

2 cups loosely packed baby arugula

1 teaspoon olive oil

2 ounces finely chopped prosciutto (about ½ cup)

1. Cook pasta according to package directions. Add peas to pasta during last 2 minutes of cooking. Drain and rinse with cold water; drain well.

2. While pasta cooks, combine mayonnaise and next 6 ingredients in a large bowl. Add pasta mixture and arugula; toss to coat.

3. Heat oil in a skillet over medium-high heat. Add prosciutto; sauté 2 minutes. Drain on paper towels. Sprinkle prosciutto over salad.

CALORIES 373; FAT 14.9g (sat 1.4g, mono 4.4g, poly 7.5g); PROTEIN 13.6g; CARB 45.7g; FIBER 3.6g; CHOL 18mg; IRON 2.8mg; SODIUM 677mg; CALC 50mg

Asian Chicken, Noodle, and Snap Pea Salad

For extra crunch, serve this Asian noodle salad over a bed of shredded napa (Chinese) cabbage. Look for toasted sesame seeds on the spice aisle of your supermarket.

Yield: 4 servings (serving size: 1½ cups)

3 ounces uncooked soba (buckwheat noodles)

1 (8-ounce) package sugar snap peas

1 red bell pepper, thinly sliced

3 cups shredded lemon-pepper rotisserie chicken

½ cup light sesame-ginger dressing (such as Newman's Own)

Toasted sesame seeds (such as McCormick) (optional)

Sliced green onions (optional)

Shredded napa (Chinese) cabbage (optional)

1. Prepare soba according to package directions. Drain.

2. While soba cooks, microwave peas in package at HIGH 1 minute. Rinse peas under cold water. Combine soba, peas, and next 3 ingredients in a large bowl; toss to combine. Garnish with sesame seeds and onions, if desired. Serve over cabbage, if desired.

CALORIES 333; FAT 8g (sat 1.7g, mono 2.3g, poly 1.6g); PROTEIN 35.2g; CARB 27.8g; FIBER 3.1g; CHOL 92mg; IRON 2.5mg; SODIUM 640mg; CALC 65mg

INGREDIENT TIP

You'll find napa cabbage in various shapes, from round to elongated. Similar in appearance to romaine lettuce, it is thin and delicate with a mild flavor.

make
ahead

Veal Paprikash

Make this dish ahead—just add the sour cream later. Boned sirloin steak can be substituted for the veal roast.

Yield: 7 servings (serving size: 1 cup stew and ¾ cup noodles)

1 tablespoon butter, divided

Cooking spray

1 (2¼-pound) lean veal tip round roast, cut into 1-inch pieces

1½ cups sliced carrot

1 cup sliced onion

1 garlic clove, minced

1.1 ounces all-purpose flour (about ¼ cup)

1 tablespoon paprika

½ teaspoon salt

½ teaspoon pepper

1 cup lower-sodium chicken broth

1 cup fat-free beef broth

½ cup dry white wine

2 bay leaves

½ cup light sour cream

5¼ cups hot cooked medium egg noodles (about 3½ cups uncooked pasta)

Chopped parsley (optional)

1. Melt 1 teaspoon butter in a Dutch oven coated with cooking spray over medium-high heat. Add veal; cook 5 minutes, browning on all sides. Remove meat from pan; set aside.

2. Melt remaining 2 teaspoons butter in pan over medium heat. Add carrot, onion, and garlic; sauté 10 minutes or until tender. Weigh or lightly spoon flour into a dry measuring cup; level with a knife. Add flour, paprika, salt, and pepper to pan; stir. Add broths, wine, and bay leaves; stir well. Return meat to pan, and bring to a boil. Cover, reduce heat, and simmer 1½ hours or until tender, stirring occasionally. Discard bay leaves. Remove from heat; stir in sour cream. Cook over low heat 5 minutes or until thoroughly heated. Serve over noodles; sprinkle with parsley, if desired.

CALORIES 423; FAT 10.4g (sat 3.8g, mono 3.5g, poly 1.6g); PROTEIN 38.4g; CARB 39.2g; FIBER 4.1g; CHOL 166mg; IRON 3.8mg; SODIUM 320mg; CALC 57mg

Farfalle with Zucchini and Prosciutto

This light and brightly flavored pasta salad will keep for up to two days in the refrigerator. Add cubed fresh mozzarella to any leftovers for a lunch to take to work.

Yield: 10 servings (serving size: about 1 cup)

1 tablespoon butter

¼ cup chopped onion

5 cups matchstick-cut zucchini (about 1 pound)

¼ cup dry white wine

¼ cup thinly sliced green onions

¼ cup reduced-fat sour cream

2 tablespoons extra-virgin olive oil

1 teaspoon kosher salt

½ teaspoon grated lemon rind

1 teaspoon fresh lemon juice

½ teaspoon freshly ground black pepper

2 ounces prosciutto, cut into thin strips (about 1 cup)

7 cups cooked farfalle (about 1 pound uncooked bow tie pasta)

1. Melt butter in a large nonstick skillet over medium-high heat. Add onion; sauté 2 minutes or until brown. Add zucchini; sauté 2 minutes. Remove zucchini mixture from pan. Add wine to pan; cook until reduced to 1 tablespoon (about 1 minute), scraping pan to loosen browned bits. Combine wine reduction, sliced green onions, and next 7 ingredients in a large bowl. Add zucchini mixture and pasta; toss to coat.

CALORIES 240; FAT 6.3g (sat 2.1g, mono 2.5g, poly 0.4g); PROTEIN 9.2g; CARB 36.5g; FIBER 2.1g; CHOL 13mg; IRON 1.8mg; SODIUM 367mg; CALC 24mg

INGREDIENT TIP

The alcohol in the wine cooks away, so it's fine for kids to enjoy this dish, or you can use broth instead.

Bow Tie Pasta with Roasted Red Bell Peppers and Cream Sauce

Roasted red peppers and a cream sauce deliver rich flavor in this quick and easy recipe. Balsamic vinegar helps balance the natural sweetness of the red bell peppers.

Yield: 6 servings

1 pound uncooked farfalle
(bow tie pasta)

2 teaspoons extra-virgin olive oil

½ cup finely chopped onion

1 (12-ounce) bottle roasted red
bell peppers, drained and coarsely
chopped

2 teaspoons balsamic vinegar

1 cup half-and-half

1 tablespoon tomato paste

⅛ teaspoon ground red pepper

1 cup (4 ounces) freshly grated
Parmigiano-Reggiano cheese,
divided

Thinly sliced fresh basil (optional)

1. Cook pasta according to package directions, omitting salt and fat.

2. Heat oil in a large skillet over medium heat. Add onion, and cook 8 minutes or until tender, stirring frequently. Add bell peppers; cook 2 minutes or until thoroughly heated. Increase heat to medium-high. Stir in vinegar; cook 1 minute or until liquid evaporates. Remove from heat; cool 5 minutes.

3. Place bell pepper mixture in a blender; process until smooth. Return bell pepper mixture to pan; cook over low heat until warm. Combine half-and-half and tomato paste in a small bowl, stirring with a whisk. Stir tomato mixture into bell pepper mixture, stirring with a whisk until well combined. Stir in ground red pepper.

4. Combine pasta and bell pepper mixture in a large bowl. Add ½ cup cheese, tossing to coat. Spoon 1⅓ cups pasta into each of 6 bowls; top each with about 1½ tablespoons cheese. Garnish with basil, if desired.

CALORIES 424; FAT 10.7g (sat 5.6g, mono 3.7g, poly 0.5g); PROTEIN 17.6g; CARB 62.9g; FIBER 3g; CHOL 32mg; IRON 2.9mg; SODIUM 383mg; CALC 222mg

Chili and Cheddar Bow Tie Casserole

If you don't have farfalle, substitute ziti, rigatoni, or even macaroni.

Yield: 6 servings (serving size: 1⅓ cups)

1 (7-ounce) can chipotle chiles in adobo sauce

1 tablespoon butter

1 cup chopped red bell pepper

½ cup diced Canadian bacon (about 2 ounces)

1 cup thinly sliced green onions

2 tablespoons all-purpose flour

1 teaspoon chili powder

½ teaspoon salt

½ teaspoon ground cumin

2¼ cups 2% reduced-fat milk

2 cups (8 ounces) reduced-fat shredded sharp cheddar cheese, divided

2 tablespoons chopped fresh cilantro

8 cups hot cooked farfalle (bow tie pasta) or other short pasta

Cooking spray

1. Preheat oven to 400°.

2. Remove 1 teaspoon adobo sauce and 1 chile from canned chiles; mince the chile. Place remaining sauce and chiles in a zip-top plastic bag; freeze for another use.

3. Melt butter in a large Dutch oven over medium-high heat. Add bell pepper and bacon; sauté 4 minutes. Add onions; sauté 1 minute. Stir in reserved adobo sauce, minced chile, flour, chili powder, salt, and cumin; cook 1 minute. Gradually add milk; cook until thick and bubbly (about 4 minutes), stirring constantly with a whisk. Remove from heat. Gradually add 1½ cups cheese and cilantro, stirring until cheese melts. Add pasta to pan; toss well.

4. Spoon pasta mixture into an 11 x 7–inch baking dish coated with cooking spray. Sprinkle remaining ½ cup cheese over pasta mixture. Bake at 400° for 15 minutes or until browned.

CALORIES 369; FAT 12.4g (sat 7.4g, mono 1.6g, poly 1g); PROTEIN 23.2g; CARB 43g; FIBER 3.1g; CHOL 44mg; IRON 1.6mg; SODIUM 758mg; CALC 472mg

Seafood Lasagna

You can always splurge on fresh crabmeat, but we tested this dish with canned Chicken of the Sea lump crabmeat and liked the results. Shrimp shells render a quick stock to flavor the sauce.

Yield: 8 servings

2 teaspoons olive oil

5 cups finely chopped mushrooms (about 1 pound)

1½ cups chopped onion

2 tablespoons chopped fresh thyme

2 garlic cloves, minced

¼ cup dry white wine

2 (6.5-ounce) cans lump crabmeat, drained

1 pound uncooked large shrimp

2 cups water

1½ teaspoons celery salt

1 teaspoon fennel seeds

1¼ cups (5 ounces) crumbled goat or feta cheese

1 cup 2% low-fat cottage cheese

¼ cup finely chopped fresh basil

1 tablespoon fresh lemon juice

1 garlic clove, minced

1.1 ounces all-purpose flour (about ¼ cup)

1 cup 1% low-fat milk

¼ cup (1 ounce) grated fresh Parmesan cheese

Cooking spray

1 (8-ounce) package precooked lasagna noodles

2 cups (8 ounces) shredded part-skim mozzarella cheese

¼ cup chopped fresh flat-leaf parsley

1. Preheat oven to 375°.

2. Heat oil in a large nonstick skillet over medium heat. Add mushrooms, onion, thyme, and 2 garlic cloves; cook 10 minutes, stirring occasionally. Add wine. Bring to a boil; cook 1½ minutes or until liquid almost evaporates. Remove from heat; stir in crabmeat. Set aside.

3. Peel and devein shrimp, reserving shells. Cut each shrimp in half lengthwise; cover and refrigerate. Combine reserved shrimp shells, 2 cups water, celery salt, and fennel seeds in a small saucepan. Bring to a boil; cook until reduced to 1½ cups shrimp stock (about 15 minutes). Strain stock through a sieve into a bowl; discard solids. Set stock aside.

4. Combine goat cheese, cottage cheese, basil, juice, and 1 garlic clove; set aside.

5. Weigh or lightly spoon flour into a dry measuring cup; level with a knife. Place flour in a small saucepan; gradually add milk, stirring with a whisk. Stir in shrimp stock; bring to a boil. Reduce heat; simmer 5 minutes or until thick. Remove from heat; stir in Parmesan cheese.

6. Spread ½ cup sauce in bottom of a 13 x 9–inch baking dish coated with cooking spray. Arrange 4 noodles, slightly overlapping, over sauce; top with one-third of goat cheese mixture, one-third of crab mixture, one-third of shrimp, ⅔ cup sauce, and ⅔ cup mozzarella. Repeat layers twice, ending with mozzarella. Bake at 375° for 40 minutes or until golden. Let stand 15 minutes. Sprinkle with parsley.

CALORIES 428; FAT 13.9g (sat 7.7g, mono 2.5g, poly 1.1g); PROTEIN 40.1g; CARB 33.6g; FIBER 3.6g; CHOL 143mg; IRON 4.1mg; SODIUM 934mg; CALC 414mg

QUICK TIP

Precooked, or oven-ready, lasagna noodles are a great way to save prep time and effort without sacrificing flavor or texture. It's best not to substitute regular noodles for precooked noodles.

Lasagna with Fall Vegetables, Gruyère, and Sage Béchamel

Although this hearty dish involves several steps, most can be done a couple of days in advance. Prepare and refrigerate the béchamel, covered, up to two days ahead. Refrigerate the mushroom–sweet potato mixture and the spinach mixture separately for up to two days.

Yield: 9 servings

Béchamel:

3 ounces all-purpose flour (about ⅔ cup)

6 cups fat-free milk

½ cup finely chopped onion

¼ cup chopped fresh sage

2 tablespoons finely chopped shallots

½ teaspoon sea salt

1 bay leaf

Filling:

1 tablespoon olive oil, divided

2½ cups finely chopped onion

3 garlic cloves, minced

1 teaspoon sea salt, divided

1 (10-ounce) package fresh spinach

8 cups chopped portobello mushroom caps (about 1½ pounds)

6 cups (½-inch) cubed peeled sweet potato (about 2½ pounds)

Cooking spray

1 cup (4 ounces) shredded Gruyère cheese

¾ cup (3 ounces) grated fresh Parmesan cheese

Noodles:

12 precooked lasagna noodles

2 cups warm water

1. Preheat oven to 450°.

2. To prepare béchamel, weigh or lightly spoon flour into dry measuring cups; level with a knife. Place flour in a Dutch oven, and gradually add milk, stirring with a whisk. Add ½ cup onion, sage, shallots, ½ teaspoon salt, and bay leaf. Bring mixture to a boil; cook 1 minute or until thick. Strain béchamel through a sieve over a bowl, and discard solids. Set béchamel aside.

3. To prepare filling, heat 1½ teaspoons olive oil in a large nonstick skillet over medium-high heat. Add 2½ cups onion and garlic; sauté 3 minutes. Add ½ teaspoon salt and spinach; sauté 2 minutes or until spinach wilts. Set aside.

4. Combine remaining 1½ teaspoons oil, remaining ½ teaspoon salt, mushrooms, and sweet potato on a jelly-roll pan coated with cooking spray. Bake at 450° for 15 minutes.

5. Combine cheeses; set aside.

6. To prepare noodles, soak noodles in 2 cups warm water in a 13 x 9–inch baking dish 5 minutes. Drain.

7. Spread ¾ cup béchamel in bottom of a 13 x 9–inch baking dish coated with cooking spray. Arrange 3 noodles over béchamel; top with half of mushroom mixture, 1½ cups béchamel, and ⅓ cup cheese mixture. Top with 3 noodles, spinach mixture, 1½ cups béchamel, and ⅓ cup cheese mixture. Top with 3 noodles, remaining mushroom mixture, 1½ cups béchamel, and 3 noodles. Spread remaining béchamel over noodles. Bake at 450° for 20 minutes. Sprinkle with remaining cheese; bake an additional 10 minutes. Let stand 10 minutes before serving.

CALORIES 418; FAT 9.5g (sat 4.5g, mono 3.2g, poly 1g); PROTEIN 22.3g; CARB 62.7g; FIBER 6.4g; CHOL 24mg; IRON 3.7mg; SODIUM 703mg; CALC 505mg

Special Occasion Lasagna

Serve this company-worthy lasagna with a tossed greens or Caesar salad and breadsticks to round out the meal.

Yield: 8 servings

1 (8-ounce) package uncooked lasagna noodles (about 9 noodles)

1⅓ cups (6 ounces) fat-free cottage cheese

¾ cup (6 ounces) ⅓-less-fat cream cheese, softened

⅔ cup (6 ounces) part-skim ricotta cheese

¼ cup (1 ounce) grated fresh Parmesan cheese

2 tablespoons minced fresh chives

1 teaspoon Dijon mustard

½ teaspoon salt

½ teaspoon dry mustard

½ teaspoon freshly ground black pepper

4 garlic cloves, minced

2 large egg whites, lightly beaten

1 large egg, lightly beaten

1 (26-ounce) jar fat-free pasta sauce, divided

Cooking spray

¼ cup (1 ounce) shredded part-skim mozzarella cheese

1. Preheat oven to 350°.

2. Cook noodles according to package directions, omitting salt and fat.

3. Combine cottage cheese, cream cheese, and ricotta cheese in a large bowl; stir to blend well. Stir in Parmesan and next 8 ingredients.

4. Spread ½ cup pasta sauce in bottom of a 13 x 9–inch baking dish coated with cooking spray. Arrange 3 noodles over pasta sauce; top with half of cheese mixture and one-third of remaining pasta sauce. Repeat layers once, ending with noodles. Spread remaining pasta sauce over noodles.

5. Bake at 350° for 20 minutes. Sprinkle with mozzarella; bake an additional 20 minutes or until cheese is melted. Remove from oven; let stand 10 minutes before serving.

CALORIES 284; FAT 8.8g (sat 5.2g, mono 2.5g, poly 0.4g); PROTEIN 15.7g; CARB 34.2g; FIBER 3.3g; CHOL 53mg; IRON 0.9mg; SODIUM 657mg; CALC 179mg

MAKE AHEAD TIP

You can make this dish ahead—just cover it, and refrigerate or freeze it after you've spread the final layer of marinara sauce.

Mac and Cheese with Roasted Tomatoes

The breadcrumb and Parmesan mixture forms a gratin-style topping that adds a light crunchiness.

Yield: 10 servings (serving size: about 1 cup)

Cooking spray

8 plum tomatoes, cut into ¼-inch-thick slices (about 2 pounds)

1 tablespoon olive oil

1 tablespoon minced fresh thyme

¾ teaspoon salt, divided

4 garlic cloves, thinly sliced

1 pound uncooked multigrain whole-wheat elbow macaroni (such as Barilla Plus)

2.25 ounces all-purpose flour (about ½ cup)

5 cups 1% low-fat milk

1½ cups (6 ounces) shredded extrasharp white cheddar cheese

1 cup (4 ounces) shredded fontina cheese

½ teaspoon black pepper

½ cup (2 ounces) grated fresh Parmesan cheese

⅓ cup dry breadcrumbs

½ teaspoon paprika

1. Preheat oven to 400°.

2. Cover a baking sheet with foil, and coat foil with cooking spray. Arrange tomato slices in a single layer on baking sheet. Drizzle oil over tomatoes. Sprinkle with thyme, ¼ teaspoon salt, and garlic. Bake at 400° for 35 minutes or until tomatoes start to dry out.

3. Cook pasta according to package directions, omitting salt and fat. Drain well.

4. Weigh or lightly spoon flour into a dry measuring cup; level with a knife. Place flour in a large Dutch oven; gradually add milk, stirring with a whisk until blended. Cook over medium heat 8 minutes or until thick and bubbly, stirring constantly with a whisk. Add cheddar, fontina, remaining ½ teaspoon salt, and pepper, stirring until cheese melts. Remove from heat. Stir in tomatoes and pasta. Spoon into a 13 x 9–inch baking dish coated with cooking spray. Combine grated Parmesan cheese, breadcrumbs, and paprika; sprinkle over pasta mixture. Bake at 400° for 25 minutes or until bubbly.

CALORIES 411; FAT 14g (sat 6.9g, mono 2.9g, poly 0.9g); PROTEIN 22.8g; CARB 49.9g; FIBER 4.7g; CHOL 39mg; IRON 2.5mg; SODIUM 638mg; CALC 414mg

MAKE AHEAD TIP

Bake this dish the night before, and reheat single servings in the microwave the next day.

Make-Ahead Cheese-and-Hamburger Casserole

The penne doesn't have to be cooked beforehand because it absorbs the liquid when refrigerated overnight. If you want to make it the same day, cook the pasta before combining it with the rest of the ingredients. For convenience, use precrumbled feta and preshredded mozzarella.

Yield: 8 servings

1 pound ground round

1 cup chopped onion

3 garlic cloves, crushed

1 (8-ounce) package presliced mushrooms

6 tablespoons tomato paste

1 teaspoon sugar

1 teaspoon dried thyme

1 teaspoon dried oregano

¼ teaspoon pepper

1 (28-ounce) can whole tomatoes, undrained and chopped

1.5 ounces all-purpose flour (about ⅓ cup)

2½ cups 2% reduced-fat milk

1 cup (4 ounces) crumbled feta cheese

¾ cup (3 ounces) shredded part-skim mozzarella cheese

4 cups uncooked penne (tube-shaped pasta)

1 tablespoon chopped fresh parsley (optional)

1. Combine first 3 ingredients in a large nonstick skillet; cook over medium-high heat until browned, stirring to crumble. Add mushrooms; cook 5 minutes or until tender. Add tomato paste and next 5 ingredients; stir well. Bring to a boil; reduce heat, and simmer, uncovered, 20 minutes. Set aside.

2. Weigh or lightly spoon flour into a dry measuring cup; level with a knife. Place flour in a medium saucepan. Gradually add milk, stirring with a whisk until blended. Place over medium heat; cook 10 minutes or until thick, stirring constantly. Stir in cheeses; cook 3 minutes or until cheeses melt, stirring constantly. Reserve ½ cup cheese sauce. Pour remaining cheese sauce, beef mixture, and pasta into a 13 x 9–inch baking dish, and stir gently. Drizzle reserved cheese sauce over pasta mixture. Cover and refrigerate 24 hours.

3. Preheat oven to 350°.

4. Bake at 350°, covered, 1 hour and 10 minutes or until thoroughly heated and pasta is tender; sprinkle with parsley, if desired.

CALORIES 412; FAT 10.8g (sat 5.5g, mono 3.2g, poly 0.9g); PROTEIN 27.5g; CARB 51.1g; FIBER 3.2g; CHOL 60mg; IRON 4.9mg; SODIUM 448mg; CALC 286mg

Baked Stuffed Shells

Yield: 6 servings (serving size: 3 stuffed shells and about 1 cup sauce)

Stuffing:

¼ cup boiling water

6 sun-dried tomatoes

1 cup (4 ounces) shredded
part-skim mozzarella cheese

¼ cup (1 ounce) grated fresh
Parmesan cheese

1 tablespoon chopped fresh parsley

¼ teaspoon freshly ground
black pepper

⅛ teaspoon salt

1 (14-ounce) package reduced-fat
firm tofu, drained

1 large egg, lightly beaten

18 cooked jumbo pasta shells

Sauce:

1 tablespoon olive oil

1¾ cups chopped onion

1 cup chopped green bell pepper

1 cup chopped red bell pepper

3 garlic cloves, minced

Cooking spray

¾ pound low-fat turkey breakfast
sausage, casings removed

¼ cup red wine

2 tablespoons no-salt-added
tomato paste

1 teaspoon dried oregano

1 teaspoon dried basil

½ teaspoon freshly ground
black pepper

⅛ teaspoon salt

1 (28-ounce) can organic crushed
tomatoes, undrained

2 tablespoons grated fresh
Parmesan cheese

1. Preheat oven to 350°.

2. To prepare stuffing, combine ¼ cup boiling water and sun-dried tomatoes in a small bowl; let stand 20 minutes or until tomatoes soften. Drain and finely chop. Combine tomatoes, mozzarella, and next 6 ingredients in a food processor; process until smooth. Spoon 2 tablespoons stuffing into each shell. Set stuffed shells aside.

3. To prepare sauce, heat oil in a large skillet over medium-high heat. Add onion, bell peppers, and garlic; sauté 6 minutes or until tender. Place onion mixture in a bowl.

4. Coat pan with cooking spray; return pan to heat. Add sausage, and cook 6 minutes or until browned, stirring to crumble. Add wine; cook until wine is reduced to 2 tablespoons (about 3 minutes). Stir in onion mixture, tomato paste, and next 5 ingredients; bring to a simmer. Cook 25 minutes or until slightly thick.

5. Spread 2 cups sauce over bottom of an 11 x 7–inch baking dish coated with cooking spray. Arrange stuffed shells in a single layer in pan; top with remaining sauce. Sprinkle 2 tablespoons Parmesan over sauce. Bake at 350° for 40 minutes or until bubbly.

CALORIES 391; FAT 13.8g (sat 4.8g, mono 5.2g, poly 2.3g); PROTEIN 27g; CARB 37.1g; FIBER 4.7g; CHOL 84mg; IRON 4mg; SODIUM 892mg; CALC 238mg

NUTRITION TIP

This recipe is a great way to mask tofu for finicky eaters. Tofu is low in calories, and it's a storehouse of vitamins and minerals, including folic acid and iron.

Eggplant Marinara Pasta Casserole

Pancetta is Italian bacon that comes in a sausagelike roll; it lends a salty bite to the marinara.

Yield: 8 servings (serving size: about 2 cups)

6 cups (½-inch) cubed eggplant (about 1 pound)

1½ teaspoons kosher salt, divided

Cooking spray

1 ounce pancetta, chopped

2 cups thinly sliced onion

1 tablespoon extra-virgin olive oil

2 garlic cloves, minced

¼ cup dry white wine

1 tablespoon chopped fresh basil

1 teaspoon chopped fresh oregano

½ teaspoon crushed red pepper

1 (28-ounce) can diced tomatoes, undrained

16 ounces uncooked penne (tube-shaped pasta)

1 cup (4 ounces) shredded fontina cheese

1 (3-inch) piece French bread baguette (2 ounces)

½ cup (2 ounces) grated fresh Parmesan cheese

1. Arrange eggplant on several layers of heavy-duty paper towels. Sprinkle eggplant with 1 teaspoon kosher salt; let stand 15 minutes. Pat dry with additional paper towels.

2. Preheat oven to 450°.

3. Arrange eggplant in a single layer on a baking sheet coated with cooking spray. Bake at 450° for 30 minutes or until lightly browned, stirring after 15 minutes. Remove from baking sheet; cool.

4. Cook pancetta in a Dutch oven over medium heat until crisp. Add onion, oil, and garlic to pan; cook 6 minutes or until onion is lightly browned, stirring frequently. Add wine to pan; cook until liquid evaporates, scraping pan to loosen browned bits. Stir in basil, oregano, remaining ½ teaspoon salt, pepper, and diced tomatoes. Bring to a simmer over medium heat; partially cover, and cook 20 minutes, stirring occasionally. Remove from heat; stir in eggplant.

5. Cook pasta according to package directions, omitting salt and fat. Drain pasta in a colander over a bowl, reserving ¼ cup cooking water. Add pasta and reserved ¼ cup cooking water to tomato mixture; stir well. Spoon pasta mixture into a 13 x 9–inch baking dish coated with cooking spray. Sprinkle evenly with fontina.

6. Place baguette in a food processor; pulse 10 times or until coarse crumbs measure 1½ cups. Add Parmesan to processor; pulse 5 times. Sprinkle breadcrumb mixture evenly over fontina.

7. Bake at 450° for 12 minutes or until cheese melts and begins to brown.

CALORIES 401; FAT 10.6g (sat 4.8g, mono 3.7g, poly 0.6g); PROTEIN 16.6g; CARB 58.5g; FIBER 5.4g; CHOL 26mg; IRON 1.7mg; SODIUM 768mg; CALC 183mg

Pork Ragout

After cooking the ragout, place it in a large heavy-duty zip-top plastic bag. Cool completely in the refrigerator, and freeze for up to one month. To reheat, place the bag in a large pot of boiling water (do not unseal bag). Cook 15 minutes or until thoroughly heated. Remove the bag from the water using tongs. While the ragout is reheating, grate the cheese, and cook the pasta according to package instructions, omitting salt and fat.

Yield: 4 servings (serving size: 1 cup ragout, 1 cup pasta, and 1 tablespoon cheese)

1 pound boneless pork loin

1 (4-ounce) link hot turkey Italian sausage

1 cup chopped onion

1 tablespoon chopped fresh or 1 teaspoon dried rosemary

¼ teaspoon salt

¼ teaspoon black pepper

¾ cup fat-free, lower-sodium chicken broth

¾ cup zinfandel or other dry red wine

1 (28-ounce) can Italian-style whole tomatoes, undrained and chopped

4 cups hot cooked penne (about 8 ounces uncooked tube-shaped pasta)

¼ cup (1 ounce) grated fresh Romano cheese

Fresh rosemary sprigs (optional)

1. Trim fat from pork; cut pork into ¼-inch cubes.

2. Remove casing from sausage. Cook sausage in a Dutch oven over medium-high heat until browned; stir to crumble. Remove sausage from pan with a slotted spoon. Add onion to pan; sauté 4 minutes or until lightly browned. Add pork, and sauté 5 minutes. Add sausage, rosemary, salt, and pepper. Stir in broth and wine, scraping pan to loosen browned bits. Bring to a boil; cook 5 minutes. Add tomatoes, and bring to a boil. Reduce heat, and simmer 30 minutes. Serve over pasta, and sprinkle with cheese. Garnish with rosemary sprigs, if desired.

CALORIES 490; FAT 12.9g (sat 4.7g, mono 4.9g, poly 2.1g); PROTEIN 36.7g; CARB 55.8g; FIBER 3.7g; CHOL 86mg; IRON 4.9mg; SODIUM 874mg; CALC 160mg

Roasted Shallot and Butternut Squash Pasta

Prepare the squash up to three days in advance. Cook the pasta, and assemble the dish to bake.

Yield: 6 servings (serving size: 1⅓ cups)

Squash:

3 tablespoons olive oil, divided

3 butternut squash, halved lengthwise and seeded (about 3½ pounds)

8 shallots, peeled (about ½ pound)

⅓ cup fat-free, lower-sodium chicken broth

2 tablespoons chopped fresh sage

2 tablespoons crème fraîche

2 tablespoons dry white wine

1 teaspoon kosher salt

¾ teaspoon freshly ground black pepper

2 garlic cloves, chopped

Pasta:

12 ounces uncooked penne (tube-shaped pasta)

⅔ cup (about 2½ ounces) shredded Asiago cheese, divided

Cooking spray

1. Preheat oven to 375°.

2. To prepare squash, drizzle 1 tablespoon oil in bottom of a roasting pan. Place squash, cut sides down, and shallots in pan. Bake, uncovered, at 375° for 45 minutes or until tender. Cool. Scoop pulp from squash; discard peels. Reserve 1½ cups pulp. Place remaining 2 tablespoons oil, remaining pulp, shallots, and next 7 ingredients in a food processor; process until smooth.

3. Reduce oven temperature to 350°.

4. To prepare pasta, cook pasta in boiling water 7 minutes or until almost tender. Drain. Combine reserved 1½ cups pulp, pureed mixture, pasta, and ⅓ cup cheese in a large bowl; stir gently. Spoon mixture into a 13 x 9–inch baking dish coated with cooking spray; cover with foil.

5. Bake at 350° for 30 minutes. Uncover; sprinkle with remaining ⅓ cup cheese. Bake 5 minutes or until cheese melts.

CALORIES 475; FAT 12.7g (sat 4.3g, mono 6.3g, poly 1g); PROTEIN 15g; CARB 80.8g; FIBER 7.5g; CHOL 16mg; IRON 4.3mg; SODIUM 386mg; CALC 276mg

INGREDIENT TIP

Look for butternut squash that has no cracks or soft spots and is heavy for its size. Butternut squash will keep for months in a cool, dry place.

Roasted Butternut Squash and Bacon Pasta

Whip up this outstanding pasta and squash casserole for an easy family meal. Mini penne pasta works well in this dish because it's about the same size as the squash. You can also use elbow macaroni, shell pasta, or orecchiette.

Yield: 5 servings

¾ teaspoon salt, divided

½ teaspoon dried rosemary

¼ teaspoon freshly ground black pepper

3 cups (1-inch) cubed peeled butternut squash

Cooking spray

6 sweet hickory-smoked bacon slices (uncooked)

1 cup thinly sliced shallots

8 ounces uncooked mini penne (tube-shaped pasta)

1.1 ounces all-purpose flour (about ¼ cup)

2 cups 2% reduced-fat milk

¾ cup (3 ounces) shredded sharp provolone cheese

⅓ cup (1½ ounces) grated fresh Parmesan cheese

1. Preheat oven to 425°.

2. Combine ¼ teaspoon salt, rosemary, and pepper. Place squash on a foil-lined baking sheet coated with cooking spray; sprinkle with salt mixture. Bake at 425° for 45 minutes or until tender and lightly browned. Increase oven temperature to 450°.

3. Cook bacon in a large nonstick skillet over medium heat until crisp. Remove bacon from pan, reserving 1½ teaspoons drippings in pan; crumble bacon. Increase heat to medium-high. Add shallots to pan; sauté 8 minutes or until tender. Combine squash mixture, bacon, and shallots; set aside.

4. Cook pasta according to package directions, omitting salt and fat. Drain well.

5. Weigh or lightly spoon flour into a dry measuring cup; level with a knife. Combine flour and remaining ½ teaspoon salt in a Dutch oven over medium-high heat. Gradually add milk, stirring constantly with a whisk; bring to a boil. Cook 1 minute or until slightly thick, stirring constantly. Remove from heat. Add provolone, stirring until cheese melts. Add pasta to cheese mixture, tossing well to combine. Spoon pasta mixture into an 11 x 7–inch baking dish lightly coated with cooking spray; top with squash mixture. Sprinkle evenly with Parmesan cheese. Bake at 450° for 10 minutes or until cheese melts and begins to brown.

CALORIES 469; FAT 14.4g (sat 7.3g, mono 4.4g, poly 0.9g); PROTEIN 22.1g; CARB 66.6g; FIBER 6.8g; CHOL 40mg; IRON 3.5mg; SODIUM 849mg; CALC 443mg

Aunt Liz's Chicken Spaghetti Casserole

This chicken spaghetti casserole is low in calories. The recipe makes two casseroles, so enjoy one for dinner and freeze the other for later. To prepare the frozen casserole, cover and bake for 55 minutes at 350°; uncover and bake an additional 10 minutes or until hot and bubbly.

Yield: 2 casseroles, 4 servings each (serving size: about 1 cup)

2 cups chopped cooked chicken breast

2 cups uncooked spaghetti, broken into 2-inch pieces (about 7 ounces)

1 cup (¼-inch-thick) sliced celery

1 cup chopped red bell pepper

1 cup chopped onion

1 cup fat-free, lower-sodium chicken broth

½ teaspoon salt

¼ teaspoon freshly ground black pepper

2 (10.75-ounce) cans condensed 30% reduced-sodium 98% fat-free cream of mushroom soup, undiluted

Cooking spray

1 cup (4 ounces) shredded cheddar cheese, divided

1. Preheat oven to 350°.

2. Combine first 5 ingredients in a large bowl. Combine broth, salt, pepper, and soup in a medium bowl, stirring with a whisk. Add soup mixture to chicken mixture; toss. Divide mixture evenly between 2 (8-inch) square or 2-quart baking dishes coated with cooking spray. Sprinkle ½ cup cheese over each casserole. Cover with foil coated with cooking spray. Bake at 350° for 35 minutes. Uncover and bake an additional 10 minutes.

CALORIES 261; FAT 7.8g (sat 3.9g, mono 2.2g, poly 1.1g); PROTEIN 19g; CARB 28g; FIBER 2.1g; CHOL 47mg; IRON 1.8mg; SODIUM 652mg; CALC 134mg

QUICK TIP

Purchase prechopped onion from your grocer's produce section to save time chopping your own.

Confetti Pasta Salad with Chicken

Here's a nice pasta salad that is great for lunch on a hot summer day. It's creamy, crunchy, and flavorful.

Yield: 8 servings (serving size: 1 cup)

½ cup water

¼ cup dry white wine

3 (4-ounce) skinless, boneless chicken breast halves

1 large garlic clove, sliced

1½ cups plain low-fat yogurt

¼ cup light mayonnaise

2½ tablespoons fresh lemon juice

1 tablespoon cider vinegar

2 teaspoons spicy brown mustard

¾ teaspoon salt

½ teaspoon dried oregano

¼ teaspoon garlic powder

¼ teaspoon black pepper

4 cups cooked tubetti or ditalini (about 1⅓ cups uncooked very short tube-shaped pasta)

½ cup chopped celery

½ cup finely chopped red bell pepper

½ cup finely chopped green bell pepper

½ cup finely chopped carrot

¼ cup chopped fresh parsley

1. Combine first 4 ingredients in a saucepan; bring to a simmer. Cover and simmer 15 minutes or until chicken is done. Remove chicken pieces from broth; cool and coarsely chop. Bring broth to a boil over high heat; cook until reduced to ¼ cup (about 5 minutes). Cool.

2. Spoon yogurt onto several layers of heavy-duty paper towels, and spread to ½-inch thickness. Cover with additional paper towels, and let stand 5 minutes. Scrape into a bowl using a rubber spatula.

3. Combine reduced broth, yogurt, mayonnaise, and next 7 ingredients in a large bowl. Stir in chicken, pasta, and remaining ingredients. Cover and chill thoroughly.

CALORIES 209; FAT 3.9g (sat 1.1g, mono 1g, poly 1.4g); PROTEIN 16g; CARB 25.7g; FIBER 1.9g; CHOL 30mg; IRON 1.8mg; SODIUM 359mg; CALC 106mg

Pumpkin Ravioli with Gorgonzola Sauce

For a new way to enjoy pumpkin in season, try these pumpkin ravioli with a rich yet mellow Gorgonzola sauce. The ravioli will float when they are perfectly cooked. Pour a chilled chardonnay to round out your meal.

Yield: 6 servings

1¼ cups canned pumpkin

2 tablespoons dry breadcrumbs

2 tablespoons grated fresh Parmesan cheese

½ teaspoon salt

½ teaspoon minced fresh sage

¼ teaspoon freshly ground black pepper

⅛ teaspoon ground nutmeg

30 round wonton wrappers

1 tablespoon cornstarch

Cooking spray

1 cup fat-free milk

1 tablespoon all-purpose flour

1½ tablespoons butter

½ cup (2 ounces) crumbled Gorgonzola cheese

3 tablespoons chopped hazelnuts, toasted

Sage sprigs (optional)

1. Spoon pumpkin onto several layers of heavy-duty paper towels, and spread to ½-inch thickness. Cover with additional paper towels; let stand 5 minutes. Scrape into a medium bowl using a rubber spatula. Stir in breadcrumbs, Parmesan, salt, minced sage, pepper, and nutmeg.

2. Working with 1 wonton wrapper at a time (cover remaining wrappers with a damp towel to keep from drying), spoon 2 teaspoons pumpkin mixture into center of wrapper. Brush edges of wrapper with water and fold in half, pressing edges firmly with fingers to form a half-moon. Place on a large baking sheet sprinkled with cornstarch. Repeat procedure with remaining wonton wrappers and pumpkin mixture.

3. Fill a large Dutch oven with water; bring to a simmer. Add half of ravioli to pan (cover remaining ravioli with a damp towel to keep from drying). Cook 4 minutes or until done (do not boil), stirring gently. Remove ravioli with a slotted spoon; lightly coat with cooking spray, and keep warm. Repeat procedure with remaining ravioli.

4. Combine milk and flour in a saucepan, stirring with a whisk. Bring to a boil; cook 1 minute or until thick, stirring constantly. Remove from heat. Add butter, stirring until butter melts. Gently stir in Gorgonzola.

5. Place 5 ravioli in each of 6 shallow bowls, and drizzle each serving with 3 tablespoons Gorgonzola mixture. Sprinkle each serving with 1½ teaspoons hazelnuts. Garnish with sage sprigs, if desired. Serve immediately.

CALORIES 250; FAT 9.1g (sat 4.5g, mono 2.7g, poly 0.7g); PROTEIN 9.5g; CARB 33g; FIBER 3.1g; CHOL 22mg; IRON 2.4mg; SODIUM 636mg; CALC 162mg

MAKE AHEAD TIP

You can assemble the ravioli a day ahead, cover with plastic wrap, and refrigerate.

Ravioli with Herbed Ricotta Filling

Yield: 4 servings

Ravioli:

¾ cup (6 ounces) whole-milk ricotta cheese

¼ cup (1 ounce) grated fresh Parmigiano-Reggiano cheese

2 tablespoons finely chopped fresh basil

½ teaspoon grated lemon rind

¼ teaspoon freshly ground black pepper

1 large egg

Classic Pasta Dough

6 quarts water

2 tablespoons fine sea salt

Sauce:

2 tablespoons extra-virgin olive oil

2 garlic cloves, minced

¼ cup chopped fresh basil

¼ cup (1 ounce) shaved fresh Parmigiano-Reggiano cheese

1. To prepare ravioli, place ricotta in a cheesecloth-lined colander; drain 30 minutes. Combine ricotta, ¼ cup Parmigiano-Reggiano, and next 4 ingredients, stirring until well combined.

2. Place 1 (15 x 3–inch) Classic Pasta Dough sheet on a lightly floured surface. Spoon 1½ teaspoons filling mixture 1½ inches from left edge in center of sheet. Spoon 1½ teaspoons filling mixture at 3-inch intervals along length of sheet. Moisten edges and in between each filling portion with water; place 1 (15 x 3–inch) pasta sheet on top, pressing to seal. Cut pasta sheet crosswise into 5 (3 x 3–inch) ravioli, trimming edges with a sharp knife or pastry wheel. Place ravioli on a lightly floured baking sheet (cover with a damp towel to prevent drying). Repeat procedure with remaining pasta sheets and filling mixture to form 20 ravioli.

3. Bring 6 quarts water and salt to a boil in an 8-quart pot. Add half of ravioli to pot; cook 1½ minutes or until no longer translucent. Remove ravioli from water with a slotted spoon. Repeat procedure with remaining ravioli.

4. To prepare sauce, heat oil in a large skillet over low heat. Add garlic to pan; cook 6 minutes or until garlic is tender. Remove from heat. Place 5 ravioli in each of 4 shallow bowls; drizzle each serving with 1½ teaspoons garlic oil. Top each serving with 1 tablespoon basil and 1 tablespoon shaved Parmigiano-Reggiano. Serve immediately.

CALORIES 394; FAT 20.5g (sat 8.1g, mono 9.1g, poly 1.6g); PROTEIN 19g; CARB 33g; FIBER 0.4g; CHOL 193mg; IRON 1.6mg; SODIUM 731mg; CALC 283mg

Classic Pasta Dough

Yield: 4 servings (serving size: 2 ounces uncooked pasta)

5.6 ounces soft wheat flour (about 1¼ cups)

⅛ teaspoon fine sea salt

2 large eggs

1. Combine flour, salt, and eggs in a food processor; pulse 10 times or until mixture is crumbly (dough will not form a ball). Turn dough out onto a lightly floured surface; knead until smooth and elastic (about 4 minutes). Shape dough into a disc; wrap with plastic wrap. Let dough stand at room temperature 20 minutes.

2. Unwrap dough. Divide dough into 8 equal portions. Working with 1 portion at a time (keep remaining dough covered to prevent drying), pass dough through pasta rollers of a pasta machine on the widest setting. Fold dough in half crosswise; fold in half again. Pass dough through rollers again. Move width gauge to next setting; pass pasta through rollers. Continue moving width gauge to narrower settings; pass dough through rollers once at each setting to form 8 (15 x 3–inch) pasta strips. Lay strips flat on a lightly floured surface; cover. Repeat procedure with remaining dough portions.

CALORIES 178; FAT 2.9g (sat 0.8g, mono 1g, poly 0.3g); PROTEIN 6.9g; CARB 30.2g; FIBER 0.2g; CHOL 106mg; IRON 0.9mg; SODIUM 107mg; CALC 21mg

Crabmeat Ravioli with Clam Sauce

Cook the sauce up to two days ahead, and reheat gently over medium-low heat before serving. Prepare a double batch of the sauce while you're at it, and freeze half to toss with pasta for a quick dinner later. You can prepare the ravioli filling up to a day in advance; fill and cook the ravioli just before serving.

Yield: 6 servings (serving size: 4 ravioli and about ⅔ cup sauce)

Sauce:

1 tablespoon olive oil

⅓ cup finely chopped onion

2 garlic cloves, minced

1 (28-ounce) can crushed tomatoes, undrained

1 (14.5-ounce) can no-salt-added diced tomatoes, undrained

2 tablespoons chopped fresh flat-leaf parsley

1 tablespoon chopped fresh oregano

¼ teaspoon salt

¼ teaspoon crushed red pepper

¼ teaspoon black pepper

1 (10-ounce) can clams, drained

Ravioli:

½ pound lump crabmeat, drained and shell pieces removed

½ cup finely chopped red bell pepper

2 tablespoons panko (Japanese breadcrumbs)

1 tablespoon chopped fresh chives

⅛ teaspoon salt

½ cup part-skim ricotta

24 round wonton wrappers or gyoza skins

1. To prepare sauce, heat olive oil in a Dutch oven over medium-high heat. Add onion, and sauté 3 minutes or until tender. Add garlic, and sauté 1 minute. Add crushed and diced tomatoes; bring to a boil. Reduce heat, and simmer 30 minutes. Add parsley, oregano, ¼ teaspoon salt, crushed red pepper, black pepper, and clams; simmer 10 minutes. Remove from heat, and set aside.

2. To prepare ravioli, combine crab, chopped red bell pepper, panko, chives, and ⅛ teaspoon salt in a medium bowl. Add ricotta; stir gently to combine. Working with 1 wonton wrapper at a time (cover remaining wrappers with a damp towel to keep them from drying), spoon about 1 tablespoon crab mixture into center of each wrapper. Moisten edges of wrapper with water. Fold in half, pinching edges together to seal and create a half-moon shape. Repeat procedure with remaining wonton wrappers and crab mixture.

3. Fill a large Dutch oven with water; bring water to a boil. Add half of ravioli; cook 4 minutes or until done. Remove ravioli from pan with a slotted spoon; keep warm. Repeat procedure with remaining ravioli. Serve ravioli immediately with sauce.

CALORIES 272; FAT 5.3g (sat 1.4g, mono 2.2g, poly 0.6g); PROTEIN 22.7g; CARB 35.7g; FIBER 5.2g; CHOL 49mg; IRON 10mg; SODIUM 706mg; CALC 171mg

GARNISH TIP

For a lovely garnish, tuck a fresh oregano sprig into each serving.

Mushroom Ravioli with Lemon-Caper Mayonnaise

We used a mixture of shiitake and button mushrooms, but you can use any combination of mushrooms. Make the ravioli ahead, and freeze them for up to two weeks. You can make the mayonnaise up to two days ahead.

Yield: 16 servings (serving size: 3 ravioli and about 1 tablespoon mayonnaise)

Mayonnaise:

¾ cup light mayonnaise

2 tablespoons fresh lemon juice

2 teaspoons capers

2 teaspoons anchovy paste or 4 anchovy fillets, mashed

Ravioli:

4 cups sliced shiitake mushroom caps (about 1 pound)

4 cups sliced button mushrooms (about 1 pound)

Cooking spray

½ cup finely chopped shallots

1½ teaspoons chopped fresh thyme leaves

3 garlic cloves, minced

⅓ cup dry sherry

2 tablespoons grated fresh Parmesan cheese

½ teaspoon salt

⅛ teaspoon black pepper

¼ cup fat-free sour cream

Cooking spray

48 wonton wrappers

1. To prepare mayonnaise, combine first 4 ingredients, stirring until smooth; cover and chill.

2. To prepare ravioli, place shiitake mushrooms in a food processor; pulse 6 times or until finely chopped. Remove from processor. Place button mushrooms in food processor; pulse 10 times or until finely chopped.

3. Heat a large nonstick skillet coated with cooking spray over medium-high heat. Add mushrooms, shallots, thyme, and garlic; sauté 15 minutes or until tender. Add sherry; bring to a boil. Cook 8 minutes or until liquid almost evaporates. Remove from heat; stir in Parmesan, salt, and pepper. Place mushroom mixture in a bowl; let stand 10 minutes. Stir in sour cream.

4. Preheat oven to 425°.

5. Coat 2 baking sheets with cooking spray. Working with 1 wonton wrapper at a time (cover remaining wrappers to prevent drying), spoon 2 teaspoons mushroom mixture into center of wrapper. Moisten edges of wrapper with water; bring 2 opposite corners together. Press edges with a fork to seal, forming a triangle.

6. Place ravioli in a single layer on prepared baking sheets; spray tops lightly with cooking spray. Bake at 425° for 14 minutes or until golden brown, turning once. Serve with mayonnaise.

CALORIES 136; FAT 4.4g (sat 0.8g, mono 1.2g, poly 2.1g); PROTEIN 4.4g; CARB 19.2g; FIBER 1g; CHOL 7mg; IRON 1.7mg; SODIUM 404mg; CALC 39mg

meat
lovers

Hamburger Stroganoff

Add a tossed green salad and sautéed red and green bell pepper strips for a satisfying family-friendly meal.

Yield: 6 servings (serving size: about ½ cup stroganoff, ⅔ cup pasta, and 1½ teaspoons parsley)

8 ounces uncooked medium egg noodles

1 teaspoon olive oil

1 pound ground beef, extra lean

1 cup prechopped onion

1 teaspoon bottled minced garlic

1 (8-ounce) package presliced cremini mushrooms

2 tablespoons all-purpose flour

1 cup fat-free, lower-sodium beef broth

1¼ teaspoons kosher salt

⅛ teaspoon black pepper

¾ cup reduced-fat sour cream

1 tablespoon dry sherry

3 tablespoons chopped fresh parsley

1. Cook pasta according to package directions, omitting salt and fat. Drain and rinse under cold water; drain.

2. Heat oil in a large nonstick skillet over medium-high heat. Add beef to pan; cook 4 minutes or until browned, stirring to crumble. Add onion, garlic, and mushrooms to pan; cook 4 minutes or until most of liquid evaporates, stirring frequently. Sprinkle with flour; cook 1 minute, stirring constantly. Stir in broth; bring to a boil. Reduce heat, and simmer 1 minute or until slightly thick. Stir in salt and pepper.

3. Remove from heat. Stir in sour cream and sherry. Serve over pasta. Sprinkle with parsley.

CALORIES 322; FAT 9.8g (sat 4.4g, mono 3.5g, poly 1.1g); PROTEIN 23.9g; CARB 35.1g; FIBER 2.1g; CHOL 82mg; IRON 3.2mg; SODIUM 541mg; CALC 70mg

Steak Tips with Peppered Mushroom Gravy

Briefly cooking the gravy with thyme sprigs saves the time of stripping the tiny leaves from the stem but still gives you the herb's woodsy flavor.

Yield: 4 servings (serving size: about ¾ cup beef mixture and ⅔ cup noodles)

2 cups uncooked egg noodles

Cooking spray

1 pound top sirloin steak, cut into ¾-inch pieces

1 tablespoon butter

2 tablespoons finely chopped shallots

1 (8-ounce) package presliced baby bella mushrooms

1 teaspoon minced garlic

1 tablespoon lower-sodium soy sauce

3 tablespoons all-purpose flour

1½ cups fat-free, lower-sodium beef broth

½ teaspoon black pepper

¼ teaspoon salt

3 fresh thyme sprigs

1 teaspoon fresh thyme leaves (optional)

1. Cook noodles according to package directions, omitting salt and fat; drain.

2. While noodles cook, heat a large nonstick skillet over medium-high heat. Coat pan with cooking spray. Add steak; sauté 5 minutes, browning on all sides. Remove from pan; cover.

3. Melt butter in pan over medium-high heat. Add shallots and mushrooms; sauté 4 minutes. Add garlic; sauté 30 seconds. Stir in soy sauce. Sprinkle flour over mushroom mixture; cook 1 minute, stirring constantly. Gradually add broth, stirring constantly. Add pepper, salt, and thyme sprigs. Bring to a boil; cook 2 minutes or until thick. Return beef to pan; cook 1 minute or until thoroughly heated. Discard thyme sprigs. Garnish with thyme leaves, if desired.

CALORIES 344; FAT 12.5g (sat 5.3g, mono 4.2g, poly 1.2g); PROTEIN 27.3g; CARB 28.7g; FIBER 1.7g; CHOL 95mg; IRON 4.3mg; SODIUM 538mg; CALC 28mg

Beef Bourguignonne with Egg Noodles

This hearty entrée actually tastes better when made a day in advance. Warm it up in a Dutch oven over medium heat until thoroughly heated, and keep warm in a slow cooker set to LOW.

Yield: 9 servings (serving size: about 1 cup beef mixture, ¾ cup noodles, and 1 teaspoon parsley)

1.5 ounces all-purpose flour (about ⅓ cup)

2 teaspoons salt, divided

¾ teaspoon freshly ground black pepper, divided

2¼ pounds beef stew meat

3 bacon slices, uncooked and chopped

1 cup chopped onion

1 cup sliced carrot

4 garlic cloves, minced

1½ cups dry red wine

1 (14-ounce) can lower-sodium beef broth

8 cups halved mushrooms (about 1½ pounds)

2 tablespoons tomato paste

2 teaspoons chopped fresh thyme

2 bay leaves

1 (16-ounce) package frozen pearl onions

7 cups hot cooked medium egg noodles (about 6 cups uncooked noodles)

3 tablespoons chopped fresh flat-leaf parsley

1. Weigh or lightly spoon flour into a dry measuring cup; level with a knife. Combine flour, 1 teaspoon salt, and ¼ teaspoon pepper in a large zip-top plastic bag. Add beef; seal and shake to coat.

2. Cook half of bacon in a large Dutch oven over medium-high heat until crisp. Remove bacon from pan with a slotted spoon; set aside. Add half of beef mixture to drippings in pan; cook 5 minutes, browning on all sides. Remove beef from pan; cover and keep warm. Repeat procedure with remaining bacon and beef mixture. Remove beef from pan; cover and keep warm.

3. Add chopped onion, sliced carrot, and minced garlic to pan; sauté 5 minutes. Stir in red wine and broth, scraping pan to loosen browned bits. Add bacon, beef, remaining 1 teaspoon salt, remaining ½ teaspoon pepper, mushrooms, tomato paste, chopped thyme, bay leaves, and pearl onions; bring to a boil. Cover, reduce heat, and simmer 45 minutes. Uncover and cook 1 hour or until beef is tender. Discard bay leaves. Serve beef mixture over noodles; sprinkle with parsley.

CALORIES 447; FAT 14.6g (sat 5.1g, mono 6.1g, poly 1.5g); PROTEIN 32.7g; CARB 45.7g; FIBER 3.9g; CHOL 117mg; IRON 6mg; SODIUM 677mg; CALC 47mg

Braised Short Ribs with Egg Noodles

The key to getting incredibly rich flavor in a sauce made from water is to create tasty browned bits on the bottom of the pan. To ensure you create those bits, use a stainless steel skillet — not a nonstick pan.

Yield: 4 servings (serving size: 1¼ cups noodles, 1 rib, and ¾ cup sauce)

1½ pounds beef short ribs, trimmed (4 ribs)

3¾ teaspoons salt, divided

½ teaspoon freshly ground black pepper

2.25 ounces all-purpose flour (about ½ cup)

2 tablespoons olive oil, divided

2½ cups water

¾ cup chopped carrot (about 1 large)

½ cup chopped onion

1 (8-ounce) package cremini mushrooms, sliced

3 garlic cloves, minced

1 tablespoon tomato paste

3 quarts water

8 ounces uncooked medium egg noodles

1. Sprinkle beef evenly with ¼ teaspoon salt and pepper; dredge in flour. Heat a large skillet over medium-high heat. Add 1 tablespoon oil to pan; swirl to coat. Add beef to pan; cook 4 minutes or until browned, turning occasionally. Add 2½ cups water, scraping pan to loosen browned bits; bring to a boil. Cover, reduce heat, and simmer 1 hour and 45 minutes or until fork-tender. Remove beef from pan; cover and keep warm. Remove cooking liquid from pan; reserve cooking liquid.

2. Heat pan over medium heat. Add remaining 1 tablespoon oil to pan; swirl to coat. Add carrot and onion; cook 4 minutes, stirring occasionally. Add mushrooms and ½ teaspoon salt; cook 5 minutes, stirring occasionally. Add garlic; cook 30 seconds, stirring constantly. Add tomato paste, and cook 30 seconds, stirring frequently. Stir in reserved cooking liquid; bring to a boil. Reduce heat, and simmer 6 minutes or until slightly thick.

3. Bring 3 quarts water and remaining 1 tablespoon salt to a boil in a large saucepan. Add noodles; cook 5 minutes or until al dente. Drain; serve noodles with ribs and sauce.

CALORIES 488; FAT 18.2g (sat 5.4g, mono 8.5g, poly 1.1g); PROTEIN 25.2g; CARB 56.3g; FIBER 4.3g; CHOL 107mg; IRON 4.4mg; SODIUM 684mg; CALC 46mg

Beef Daube Provençal

This classic French braised beef, red wine, and vegetable stew is simple and delicious. The flavor and texture allow you to keep it warm for your guests. Buy a whole-grain baguette, bagged salad greens, and bottled vinaigrette to round out the meal. To make in a slow cooker, prepare through Step 2. Place beef mixture in an electric slow cooker. Cover and cook on HIGH 5 hours.

Yield: 6 servings (serving size: about ¾ cup stew and ½ cup noodles)

2 teaspoons olive oil

12 garlic cloves, crushed

1 (2-pound) boneless chuck roast, trimmed and cut into 2-inch cubes

1½ teaspoons salt, divided

½ teaspoon freshly ground black pepper, divided

1 cup red wine

2 cups chopped carrot

1½ cups chopped onion

½ cup lower-sodium beef broth

1 tablespoon tomato paste

1 teaspoon chopped fresh rosemary

1 teaspoon chopped fresh thyme

Dash of ground cloves

1 (14½-ounce) can diced tomatoes, undrained

1 bay leaf

3 cups cooked medium egg noodles (about 4 cups uncooked noodles)

1. Preheat oven to 300°.

2. Heat oil in a small Dutch oven over low heat. Add garlic; cook 5 minutes or until garlic is fragrant, stirring occasionally. Remove garlic with a slotted spoon, and set aside. Increase heat to medium-high. Add beef to pan; sprinkle with ½ teaspoon salt and ¼ teaspoon pepper. Cook 5 minutes, browning on all sides. Remove beef from pan. Add wine to pan; bring to a boil, scraping pan to loosen browned bits. Add garlic, beef, remaining 1 teaspoon salt, remaining ¼ teaspoon pepper, carrot, and next 8 ingredients, and bring to a boil.

3. Cover and bake at 300° for 2½ hours or until beef is tender. Discard bay leaf. Serve over noodles.

CALORIES 367; FAT 12.8g (sat 4.3g, mono 5.8g, poly 0.9g); PROTEIN 29.1g; CARB 33.4g; FIBER 3.9g; CHOL 105mg; IRON 4.3mg; SODIUM 776mg; CALC 76mg

Beef Carbonnade

A staff favorite, this easy recipe relies on the age-old technique of braising, in which less tender cuts of meat, along with aromatic vegetables, slowly cook in liquid. The fork-tender beef will melt in your mouth.

Yield: 6 servings (serving size: 1 cup beef mixture and 1 cup noodles)

2 slices bacon, finely diced

2 pounds lean, boneless chuck roast, cut into 1-inch cubes

½ teaspoon salt

½ teaspoon pepper

1 garlic clove, minced

5 cups thinly sliced onion

3 tablespoons all-purpose flour

1 cup beef broth

2 teaspoons white wine vinegar

½ teaspoon sugar

½ teaspoon dried thyme

1 bay leaf

1 (12-ounce) can light beer

6 cups cooked egg noodles (about 6 cups uncooked)

1. Preheat oven to 325°.

2. Cook bacon in a large Dutch oven over medium heat until crisp; remove bacon with a slotted spoon, reserving drippings in pan. Set bacon aside. Cook beef, salt, and pepper in drippings over medium-high heat 3 minutes, browning beef well on all sides. Add garlic; cook 30 seconds. Remove beef with a slotted spoon; set aside.

3. Add onion to pan; cover and cook 10 minutes, stirring occasionally. Stir in flour, and cook 2 minutes. Add broth and next 5 ingredients, and bring to a boil. Return bacon and beef to pan. Cover and bake at 325° for 2 hours or until beef is tender; discard bay leaf. Serve over noodles.

CALORIES 545; FAT 15.5g (sat 5.4g, mono 6.2g, poly 1.8g); PROTEIN 43.8g; CARB 52.3g; FIBER 5.5g; CHOL 158mg; IRON 7.1mg; SODIUM 644mg; CALC 58mg

INGREDIENT TIP

Egg noodles differ from regular pasta in that they contain egg or egg yolks, and they have a slightly

higher fat content than other noodles. Look for egg noodles in the pasta or bulk food section of natural food or grocery stores.

Roasted Tomato–Beef Goulash with Caraway

Sheryl Chomak of Beaverton, Oregon, says that Hungarian goulash was a family favorite when she was growing up. Here's an updated version of her mom's recipe with fresh vegetables. Replacing plain tomato sauce with roasted diced tomatoes improves the taste and texture of the gravy.

Yield: 8 servings (serving size: ½ cup goulash and ½ cup noodles)

2 pounds bottom round roast, trimmed and cut into 1-inch pieces

1 teaspoon kosher salt, divided

½ teaspoon freshly ground black pepper

2 teaspoons canola oil

2 tablespoons paprika, divided

1 to 2 teaspoons caraway seeds

1¼ cups coarsely chopped onion (about 1 large)

½ cup finely chopped celery

½ cup finely chopped carrot

1 tablespoon minced garlic

1 (14.5-ounce) can fire-roasted diced tomatoes, undrained (such as Muir Glen)

4 cups cooked medium egg noodles (about 2½ cups uncooked pasta)

Chopped fresh parsley (optional)

1. Sprinkle beef with ½ teaspoon salt and pepper.

2. Heat oil in a large Dutch oven over medium-high heat. Add beef to pan; cook 3 minutes or until browned on all sides. Add 1 tablespoon paprika and caraway seeds. Reduce heat to medium, and cook 2 minutes, stirring constantly. Stir in remaining ½ teaspoon salt, remaining 1 tablespoon paprika, onion, celery, carrot, and garlic; cook 5 minutes, stirring occasionally. Add tomatoes; bring to a boil. Cover, reduce heat, and simmer 1½ hours or until beef is tender. Serve over noodles. Garnish with parsley, if desired.

CALORIES 299; FAT 8.5g (sat 2.3g, mono 3.6g, poly 1.2g); PROTEIN 27.2g; CARB 27.6g; FIBER 2.9g; CHOL 91mg; IRON 4.5mg; SODIUM 403mg; CALC 41mg

Asparagus-and-Ham Casserole

Because of the delicate flavors in this dish, we prefer using a mild baked ham rather than a smoked one.

Yield: 6 servings (serving size: 1 cup)

1 (1-ounce) slice white bread

3¾ cups uncooked extra-broad egg noodles

2½ cups (1½-inch) sliced asparagus

1.1 ounces all-purpose flour (about ¼ cup)

½ teaspoon dried thyme

¼ teaspoon salt

⅛ teaspoon black pepper

1 cup whole milk

1 cup fat-free, lower-sodium chicken broth

1 tablespoon butter

¾ cup finely chopped onion

1 tablespoon fresh lemon juice

1½ cups (½-inch) cubed ham (about 8 ounces)

¼ cup chopped fresh flat-leaf parsley

2 tablespoons grated fresh Parmesan cheese

1. Preheat oven to 450°.

2. Place bread in a food processor, and pulse 10 times or until coarse crumbs form to measure ½ cup.

3. Cook pasta in boiling water 7 minutes, omitting salt and fat. Add asparagus; cook 1 minute. Drain.

4. Weigh or lightly spoon flour into a dry measuring cup, and level with a knife. Place flour, thyme, salt, and pepper in medium bowl; gradually add milk and broth, stirring with a whisk until well blended. Melt butter in a medium saucepan over medium-high heat. Add onion; sauté 4 minutes. Add milk mixture; cook until thick (about 4 minutes), stirring constantly. Remove from heat, and stir in juice. Combine pasta mixture, milk mixture, ham, and parsley in a large bowl; spoon into a 2-quart casserole. Sprinkle with breadcrumbs and cheese.

5. Bake at 450° for 10 minutes or until filling is bubbly and topping is golden.

CALORIES 250; FAT 7.1g (sat 3.4g, mono 2.4g, poly 0.7g); PROTEIN 16g; CARB 30.9g; FIBER 2.7g; CHOL 52mg; IRON 2.6mg; SODIUM 835mg; CALC 114mg

Smoky Meatballs in Serrano Ham–Tomato Sauce

This zesty one-dish meal combines beef, a great source of zinc, with vitamin C–rich tomatoes. To prepare ahead, cook meatballs, cool, and freeze in a zip-top plastic bag for up to one month. When you're ready to serve the dish, defrost the meatballs in the refrigerator, and sauté the ham. Follow the recipe, adding the thawed meatballs along with the tomatoes to the cooked onion mixture. Serve with a bold and bright red Rioja wine.

Yield: 4 servings

1 (1½-ounce) slice white bread

1 pound 92% lean ground beef

¼ cup finely chopped onion

2 tablespoons chopped fresh flat-leaf parsley

½ teaspoon kosher salt

½ teaspoon smoked paprika

1½ teaspoons minced garlic

¼ teaspoon freshly ground black pepper

1 large egg

2 teaspoons olive oil, divided

2 ounces serrano ham, finely chopped

Cooking spray

2 cups chopped onion

1¼ cups chopped red bell pepper

1½ teaspoons minced fresh garlic

½ cup dry sherry

1 (28-ounce) can no-salt-added whole peeled tomatoes, undrained and chopped

4 cups hot cooked fettuccine (about 8 ounces uncooked pasta)

¼ cup (1 ounce) finely shredded aged Manchego cheese

Chopped fresh flat-leaf parsley (optional)

1. Place bread in a food processor; pulse 12 times or until coarse crumbs measure ½ cup. Combine breadcrumbs, beef, and next 7 ingredients in a bowl. Using wet hands, shape mixture into 20 (about 2 tablespoons each) meatballs. Set aside.

2. Heat 1 teaspoon oil in a large Dutch oven over medium heat. Add ham to pan, and cook 3 minutes or until well browned, stirring frequently. Transfer to a large bowl. Add remaining 1 teaspoon oil to pan. Add meatballs; cook 5 minutes or until browned, turning often. Add meatballs to ham in bowl. Coat pan with cooking spray. Add onion, bell pepper, and garlic to pan; cook 5 minutes or until tender, stirring often. Add sherry; cook 3 minutes or until liquid almost evaporates, scraping pan to loosen browned bits. Add tomatoes and meatball mixture; bring to a boil. Cover, reduce heat, and simmer 30 minutes or until sauce is slightly thick. Remove from heat, and keep warm.

3. Place 1 cup pasta in each of 4 shallow bowls; top each serving with 5 meatballs, ¾ cup sauce, and 1 tablespoon shredded Manchego cheese. Garnish with additional parsley, if desired.

CALORIES 559; FAT 17.6g (sat 6.6g, mono 7.2g, poly 1.2g); PROTEIN 38.5g; CARB 61.3g; FIBER 4.7g; CHOL 128mg; IRON 6mg; SODIUM 704mg; CALC 180mg

Fettuccine Alfredo with Bacon

When you're short on time and the ingredient list is short, make every ingredient the freshest and best you can find. A real wood-smoked bacon imparts lots of flavor: Applewood is mild and slightly sweet, while hardwood, such as hickory, is more assertive.

Yield: 4 servings (serving size: about 1 cup)

1 (9-ounce) package refrigerated fresh fettuccine

2 slices applewood-smoked bacon, chopped

1 teaspoon minced garlic

1 tablespoon all-purpose flour

1 cup 1% low-fat milk

⅔ cup (about 2½ ounces) grated fresh Parmigiano-Reggiano cheese

½ teaspoon salt

2 tablespoons chopped fresh parsley

½ teaspoon freshly ground black pepper

1. Cook pasta according to package directions, omitting salt and fat. Drain in a colander over a bowl, reserving ¼ cup cooking liquid.

2. While pasta cooks, cook bacon in a large nonstick skillet over medium-high heat 4 minutes or until crisp, stirring occasionally. Remove bacon from pan, reserving drippings. Add garlic to drippings in pan; sauté 1 minute, stirring constantly. Sprinkle flour over garlic; cook 30 seconds, stirring constantly. Gradually add milk, stirring constantly; cook 2 minutes or until bubbly and slightly thick, stirring constantly. Reduce heat to low. Gradually add cheese, stirring until cheese melts. Stir in salt and reserved ¼ cup cooking liquid. Add hot pasta to pan; toss well to combine. Sprinkle with bacon, parsley, and pepper.

CALORIES 339; FAT 11.7g (sat 5g, mono 3.8g, poly 0.7g); PROTEIN 17.3g; CARB 38.4g; FIBER 2g; CHOL 22mg; IRON 0.5mg; SODIUM 833mg; CALC 291mg

Cinnamon-Beef Noodles

In this classic version of red-cooking, the meat is simmered in a soy sauce–based mixture for a long time until tender. Seasonings such as ginger, garlic, and cinnamon provide extra flavor. This method can be used to cook a variety of meats, including pork, lamb, chicken, and duck.

Yield: 8 servings (serving size: 1 cup beef mixture and ½ cup noodles)

5 cups water

1½ cups rice wine or sake

¾ cup lower-sodium soy sauce

¼ cup sugar

2 teaspoons vegetable oil

2 pounds beef stew meat, cut into 1½-inch cubes

8 green onions, cut into 1-inch pieces

6 garlic cloves, crushed

2 cinnamon sticks

1 (1-inch) piece peeled fresh ginger, thinly sliced

1 (10-ounce) package fresh spinach, chopped

4 cups hot cooked wide lo mein noodles or vermicelli (about 8 ounces uncooked pasta)

1. Combine first 4 ingredients in a large bowl; stir with a whisk. Set aside.

2. Heat 1 teaspoon oil in a large Dutch oven over medium-high heat; add half of beef, browning on all sides. Remove from pan. Repeat procedure with remaining oil and beef. Return beef to pan; add water mixture, onions, garlic, cinnamon, and ginger. Bring to a boil; cover, reduce heat, and simmer 2 hours or until beef is tender. Discard ginger slices and cinnamon. Stir in spinach; cook 3 minutes or until wilted. Serve over noodles.

CALORIES 403; FAT 6.2g (sat 2.3g, mono 3.3g, poly 1.3g); PROTEIN 30.5g; CARB 50.4g; FIBER 2.9g; CHOL 44mg; IRON 5.2mg; SODIUM 1080mg; CALC 80mg

FLAVOR TIP

Cinnamon sticks add a subtle sweet heat, while the warm, slightly woody flavor of ginger adds an herbal liveliness. Garlic is very pungent, and the more it's chopped, the stronger it tastes. Together these seasonings provide a kick of flavor.

Osso Buco with Gremolata

Inexpensive veal shanks become a succulent meal in the slow cooker. Even if you aren't an anchovy lover, don't omit the anchovy paste—it adds immeasurably to the flavor. Use the remaining broth mixture in soups and stews.

Yield: 8 servings (serving size: 3 ounces veal, 1 cup pasta, ½ cup broth mixture, and 1 tablespoon gremolata)

Osso Buco:

3 ounces all-purpose flour (about ⅔ cup)

¾ teaspoon freshly ground black pepper, divided

½ teaspoon kosher salt, divided

6 veal shanks, trimmed (about 5 pounds)

2 teaspoons butter

2 teaspoons olive oil

2 cups coarsely chopped red onion

1½ cups chopped celery

6 garlic cloves, minced

4 cups beef broth

2 cups dry white wine

1 tablespoon chopped fresh rosemary

1 tablespoon anchovy paste

Gremolata:

½ cup chopped fresh flat-leaf parsley

1 tablespoon grated lemon rind

2 garlic cloves, minced

Remaining Ingredient:

8 cups hot cooked pappardelle pasta (about 1 pound uncooked wide ribbon pasta)

1. To prepare osso buco, combine flour, ¼ teaspoon pepper, and ¼ teaspoon salt in a shallow dish. Dredge veal in flour mixture.

2. Heat 1 teaspoon butter and 1 teaspoon oil in a large skillet over medium heat. Add half of veal; cook 6 minutes, browning on both sides. Place browned veal in a large electric slow cooker. Repeat procedure with remaining butter, oil, and veal.

3. Add onion and celery to pan; sauté 5 minutes over medium-high heat or until tender. Add 6 garlic cloves to pan; sauté 1 minute. Stir in broth, wine, rosemary, and anchovy paste, scraping pan to loosen browned bits. Bring to a boil; cook 4 minutes. Pour over veal.

4. Cover and cook on LOW 9 hours or until done. Sprinkle veal with remaining ½ teaspoon pepper and remaining ¼ teaspoon salt. Remove veal from cooker; cool slightly.

5. To prepare gremolata, combine parsley, lemon rind, and 2 garlic cloves. Place 1 cup pasta in each of 8 pasta bowls. Top each serving with ⅔ cup veal and ½ cup broth mixture. Reserve remaining broth mixture for another use. Sprinkle each serving with 1 tablespoon gremolata.

CALORIES 443; FAT 12.2g (sat 4.1g, mono 4.9g, poly 1.1g); PROTEIN 54.9g; CARB 15.9g; FIBER 1.8g; CHOL 200mg; IRON 3.3mg; SODIUM 485mg; CALC 94mg

Chili Mac

This kid-friendly classic is a staple for school nights, and you can substitute whatever small pasta or cheese you have on hand. For additional convenience, use frozen chopped onion and chopped green bell pepper. Leftovers are even better the next day.

Yield: 8 servings (serving size: 1 cup beef mixture and 2 tablespoons cheese)

1 pound ground round

½ cup chopped onion

½ cup chopped green bell pepper

3 garlic cloves, minced

2 cups cooked elbow macaroni (about 4 ounces uncooked)

½ cup water

1 tablespoon chili powder

1 teaspoon ground cumin

¼ teaspoon black pepper

1 (14.5-ounce) can whole tomatoes, undrained and chopped

1 (15-ounce) can kidney beans, drained

1 (8¾-ounce) can whole-kernel corn, drained

1 (8-ounce) can tomato sauce

1 (6-ounce) can tomato paste

1 cup (4 ounces) shredded sharp cheddar cheese

1. Cook first 4 ingredients in a large Dutch oven over medium-high heat until browned, stirring to crumble beef. Drain well; wipe drippings from pan with paper towels. Return beef mixture to pan; stir in macaroni and next 9 ingredients. Bring to a boil; cover, reduce heat, and simmer 20 minutes, stirring occasionally. Spoon onto each of 8 plates; top with cheese.

CALORIES 295; FAT 9.2g (sat 4.4g, mono 3g, poly 0.8g); PROTEIN 22.6g; CARB 32.5g; FIBER 4.2g; CHOL 50mg; IRON 4.3mg; SODIUM 529mg; CALC 151mg

QUICK TIP

Why use two pans when you can use one? A quick wipe with a paper towel removes any

grease from the cooked beef, and your pan is good to go for the remainder of the recipe.

Whole-Wheat Pasta with Sausage, Leeks, and Fontina

Whole-wheat pasta makes this hearty. The flavors meld and provide just enough of each element in every bite to keep you wanting more.

Yield: 6 servings (serving size: 1⅔ cups)

6 quarts water

2½ teaspoons salt, divided

1 pound uncooked whole-wheat penne or rigatoni

1 tablespoon olive oil

1 (4-ounce) link sweet Italian sausage

2 cups chopped leek

4 cups shredded Savoy cabbage (about 9½ ounces)

1 cup fat-free, lower-sodium chicken broth

¼ teaspoon freshly ground black pepper

½ cup (2 ounces) shredded fontina cheese

1. Bring 6 quarts water and 2 teaspoons salt to a boil in a large stockpot. Stir in pasta; partially cover, and return to a boil, stirring frequently. Cook 8 minutes or until pasta is almost al dente, stirring occasionally. Drain.

2. While pasta cooks, heat olive oil in a Dutch oven over medium-high heat. Remove casing from sausage. Add sausage to Dutch oven; cook 2 minutes or until lightly browned, stirring to crumble. Add leek; cook 2 minutes or until leek is soft, stirring frequently. Add cabbage; cook 2 minutes or until cabbage wilts, stirring frequently. Add remaining ½ teaspoon salt, broth, and pepper; bring to a boil. Reduce heat, and simmer 15 minutes or until vegetables are very tender.

3. Add pasta to Dutch oven, tossing well to coat; bring to a boil. Reduce heat, and cook 1 minute, stirring constantly, or until pasta is al dente. Remove from heat; stir in cheese. Serve immediately.

CALORIES 385; FAT 8.9g (sat 3.2g, mono 3.8g, poly 1.2g); PROTEIN 17.3g; CARB 64.3g; FIBER 8.3g; CHOL 18mg; IRON 3.8mg; SODIUM 658mg; CALC 119mg

Sirloin Steak and Pasta Salad

Salt-free garlic-pepper seasons juicy steak. We recommend using sirloin, but flank steak works great, too.

Yield: 4 servings (serving size: about 1½ cups)

3 quarts water

2 cups uncooked penne or mostaccioli (tube-shaped pasta)

¼ pound green beans, trimmed

1 (¾-pound) boneless sirloin steak, trimmed

1 tablespoon salt-free garlic-pepper blend (such as Spice Hunter)

1½ cups thinly sliced red onion

1½ cups thinly sliced red bell pepper

¼ cup chopped fresh basil

3 tablespoons Dijon mustard

2 tablespoons balsamic vinegar

1 teaspoon extra-virgin olive oil

1 teaspoon bottled minced garlic

¼ teaspoon salt

¼ teaspoon black pepper

¼ cup (1 ounce) crumbled blue cheese

1. Preheat broiler.

2. While broiler preheats, bring 3 quarts water to a boil in a large Dutch oven. Add pasta; cook 5½ minutes. Add beans, and cook 3 minutes or until pasta is done. Drain and rinse with cold water. Drain well.

3. Sprinkle steak with garlic-pepper blend. Place on a broiler pan; broil 3 inches from heat 10 minutes or until desired degree of doneness, turning after 5 minutes. Let stand 5 minutes. Cut steak diagonally across grain into thin slices.

4. Combine onion and next 8 ingredients in a large bowl. Add pasta mixture and beef slices; toss well to coat. Sprinkle with cheese.

CALORIES 437; FAT 11.8g (sat 4.3g, mono 4.5g, poly 0.8g); PROTEIN 29.4g; CARB 54.4g; FIBER 4.4g; CHOL 54mg; IRON 4.5mg; SODIUM 582mg; CALC 100mg

FLAVOR TIP

Dijon mustard is common as a sandwich spread, but it also works wonders in sauces and vinaigrettes, as in this pasta salad recipe. It not only adds flavor but also helps bind the ingredients.

Rice Noodles with Sesame-Ginger Flank Steak

You'll love this combination of flank steak, crisp vegetables, and rice noodles coated in a fragrant Chinese-style sauce.

Yield: 6 servings (serving size: 1⅓ cups)

⅓ cup rice vinegar

3 tablespoons lower-sodium soy sauce

1 tablespoon hoisin sauce

2 teaspoons cornstarch

1½ teaspoons sugar

2 teaspoons grated peeled fresh ginger

¼ teaspoon salt

3 garlic cloves, minced

2 teaspoons dark sesame oil

1 (1-pound) flank steak, trimmed and cut into ¼-inch strips

1½ cups shredded carrot

1½ cups sugar snap peas, trimmed

1 cup (¼-inch) sliced red bell pepper strips

½ cup fresh bean sprouts

4 cups hot cooked rice noodles (about 8 ounces uncooked noodles)

½ cup chopped green onions

1 tablespoon sesame seeds, toasted

1. Combine first 8 ingredients, stirring until sugar dissolves.

2. Heat a large nonstick skillet over medium-high heat. Add 1 teaspoon oil to pan. Add half of steak; sauté 4 minutes or until browned. Remove steak from pan. Repeat procedure with remaining oil and steak. Add vinegar mixture, carrot, peas, bell pepper, and sprouts to pan; cook 3 minutes, stirring frequently. Return steak to pan. Add noodles; cook 1 minute, stirring constantly. Sprinkle with onions and sesame seeds.

CALORIES 369; FAT 10.4g (sat 3.7g, mono 4g, poly 1.4g); PROTEIN 24.3g; CARB 42.9g; FIBER 4.4g; CHOL 51mg; IRON 3.1mg; SODIUM 542mg; CALC 63mg

QUICK TIP

To save time, look for presliced vegetables in the produce section of your supermarket.

Korean-Style Beef Skewers with Rice Noodles

Find the noodles and sambal oelek on the ethnic aisle of your supermarket or in an Asian market.

Yield: 4 servings (serving size: 2 skewers and ½ cup noodles)

1 (1-pound) top sirloin steak, trimmed

6 tablespoons lower-sodium soy sauce

⅓ cup sugar

1½ tablespoons sambal oelek (chile paste with garlic, such as Huy Fong)

1 tablespoon canola oil

1 tablespoon fresh lime juice

4 garlic cloves, minced

½ cup water

8 ounces wide rice sticks

3 tablespoons thinly sliced green onions

1. Preheat grill to medium-high heat.

2. Cut steak diagonally across grain into thin slices. Combine steak and next 6 ingredients in a zip-top bag. Add beef to bag; seal. Marinate at room temperature 30 minutes, turning once. Remove steak from bag; reserve marinade. Thread steak evenly onto 8 (8-inch) skewers. Grill 2 minutes on each side or until desired degree of doneness. Combine reserved marinade and ½ cup water in a small saucepan; bring to a boil. Cook 1 minute.

3. Soak noodles in boiling water until tender; drain. Place noodles in a large bowl. Pour reserved marinade mixture over noodles, and sprinkle with onions; toss. Serve with skewers.

CALORIES 303; FAT 8g (sat 2g, mono 3.8g, poly 1.2g); PROTEIN 23.9g; CARB 33.3g; FIBER 0.5g; CHOL 42mg; IRON 2.3mg; SODIUM 850mg; CALC 34mg

FLAVOR TIP

Sambal oelek (chile paste with garlic) is a Chinese condiment often added to stews as a flavoring. It's essentially pureed fresh chiles, but some varieties have bean paste added. This thin sauce has intense heat.

Baked Rigatoni with Beef

Slightly undercook the pasta for this classic hamburger casserole because it cooks again in the oven.

Yield: 8 servings (serving size: 1 cup)

4 cups Tomato Sauce

1 pound ground round

4 cups cooked rigatoni (about 2½ cups uncooked pasta)

1½ cups (6 ounces) shredded part-skim mozzarella cheese, divided

Cooking spray

¼ cup (1 ounce) grated fresh Parmesan cheese

1. Prepare Tomato Sauce.

2. Preheat oven to 350°.

3. Cook beef in a large nonstick skillet over medium-high heat until browned; stir to crumble. Drain well. Combine beef, rigatoni, Tomato Sauce, and 1 cup mozzarella in an 11 x 7–inch baking dish coated with cooking spray. Top with ½ cup mozzarella and Parmesan. Bake at 350° for 20 minutes or until thoroughly heated.

CALORIES 305; FAT 9.6g (sat 4.3g, mono 3.5g, poly 0.7g); PROTEIN 24g; CARB 30.5g; FIBER 2.3g; CHOL 50mg; IRON 3.5mg; SODIUM 438mg; CALC 232mg

Tomato Sauce

Canned tomatoes and other standard pantry ingredients team up for a quick tomato sauce that'll beat the jarred variety any day. Use it anywhere you might use store-bought, such as on pasta, in lasagna, or over polenta. This sauce will freeze well for up to three months. Place it in an airtight container or zip-top plastic bag and freeze.

Yield: 8 cups (serving size: 1 cup)

1 tablespoon olive oil

1½ cups chopped onion

1 cup chopped green bell pepper

1 teaspoon dried oregano

4 garlic cloves, minced

½ cup dry red wine

1 teaspoon dried basil

½ teaspoon salt

¼ teaspoon black pepper

2 (28-ounce) cans whole plum tomatoes, undrained and chopped

1 (6-ounce) can tomato paste

2 bay leaves

1. Heat oil in a large saucepan over medium-high heat. Add onion, bell pepper, oregano, and garlic; cook 5 minutes or until vegetables are tender, stirring occasionally.

2. Add wine and remaining ingredients, and bring to a boil. Reduce heat, and simmer 30 minutes. Remove bay leaves.

CALORIES 93; FAT 2.4g (sat 0.4g, mono 1.4g, poly 0.5g); PROTEIN 3.3g; CARB 17.1g; FIBER 3.3g; CHOL 0mg; IRON 2.4mg; SODIUM 487mg; CALC 77mg

French Onion–Beef Bowl

Easy, delicious, and makes great leftovers, too! It's a wonderful winter recipe that will win rave reviews.

Yield: 6 servings (serving size: ⅔ cup noodles, about 1⅔ cups broth mixture, ⅓ cup croutons, and about 1 tablespoon cheese)

1½ pounds boned sirloin steak, trimmed and thinly sliced

½ cup chopped fresh parsley

2 tablespoons balsamic vinegar

2 teaspoons chopped fresh or ½ teaspoon dried thyme

4 garlic cloves, crushed

1 tablespoon butter

6 cups vertically sliced onion (about 3 onions)

1 teaspoon sugar

3 tablespoons all-purpose flour

3 cups water

1 cup dry white wine

1 (14-ounce) can fat-free, lower-sodium chicken broth

1 (10½-ounce) can beef consommé

1 tablespoon Worcestershire sauce

½ teaspoon black pepper

¼ teaspoon salt

4 cups hot cooked soba noodles (about 8 ounces uncooked buckwheat noodles)

2 cups garlic-flavored croutons

½ cup (2 ounces) shredded Gruyère or Jarlsberg cheese

1. Combine first 5 ingredients in a large zip-top plastic bag. Seal and marinate in refrigerator 1 to 4 hours.

2. Melt butter in a large Dutch oven over medium-high heat. Add onion and sugar, and cook 10 minutes or until golden brown, stirring frequently. Reduce heat to medium. Cover and cook 10 minutes, stirring frequently. Stir flour into onion mixture, and cook, uncovered, 2 minutes. Add 3 cups water, wine, broth, and consommé, stirring with a whisk. Bring to a boil; partially cover, reduce heat, and simmer 20 minutes. Add beef mixture, Worcestershire, pepper, and salt; cook, uncovered, 5 minutes. Place noodles into each of 6 bowls; top with broth mixture, croutons, and cheese.

CALORIES 526; FAT 14.9g (sat 6.1g, mono 5.4g, poly 2g); PROTEIN 37.7g; CARB 56.1g; FIBER 2.6g; CHOL 94mg; IRON 5.2mg; SODIUM 733mg; CALC 159mg

Spaghetti with Meat Sauce

Forget spaghetti with marinara. Real meat lovers want a meat sauce with their spaghetti, and this recipe delivers. Be sure to use a good red wine for great flavor. Serve with a side salad and breadsticks.

Yield: 6 servings (serving size: about 1 cup pasta and ⅔ cup sauce)

12 ounces uncooked spaghetti

¾ pound ground sirloin

1 cup chopped onion

1½ teaspoons bottled minced garlic

¾ cup dry red wine

1 (26-ounce) jar low-fat spaghetti sauce (such as Healthy Choice Traditional Pasta Sauce)

⅔ cup 2% reduced-fat milk

½ teaspoon salt

¼ teaspoon black pepper

1. Cook pasta according to package directions, omitting salt and fat.

2. While pasta cooks, heat a large nonstick skillet over medium-high heat. Add beef; cook until browned, stirring to crumble. Drain beef, and set aside.

3. Add onion and garlic to pan; sauté 3 minutes. Add wine; cook 3 minutes or until liquid almost evaporates.

4. Stir in beef and spaghetti sauce; bring to a boil. Reduce heat, and simmer 5 minutes, stirring occasionally. Stir in milk, salt, and pepper; cook 3 minutes, stirring occasionally. Serve sauce over pasta.

CALORIES 401; FAT 6.9g (sat 1.8g, mono 2.9g, poly 1.1g); PROTEIN 22.8g; CARB 60.1g; FIBER 4.9g; CHOL 37mg; IRON 4.7mg; SODIUM 544mg; CALC 77mg

Soba with Marinated Beef and Tomatoes

This Asian-inspired recipe is easy to prepare and yields excellent results. If you'd like, consider adding mushrooms in lieu of some of the tomatoes or toss in some green beans for an added splash of color.

Yield: 4 servings (serving size: 1½ cups)

1 (1-pound) flank steak, trimmed

1 teaspoon cornstarch

2 teaspoons vegetable oil, divided

1 teaspoon water

1 teaspoon whiskey (optional)

½ teaspoon lower-sodium soy sauce

¼ teaspoon salt

10 ounces uncooked soba (buckwheat noodles) or vermicelli

½ cup (1-inch) sliced green onions

½ cup fat-free, lower-sodium chicken broth

½ teaspoon sugar

4 plum tomatoes, quartered (about ½ pound)

1 teaspoon oyster sauce

1 garlic clove, crushed

1. Cut steak diagonally across grain into thin slices. Combine cornstarch, 1 teaspoon oil, 1 teaspoon water, whiskey, if desired, soy sauce, and salt in a large zip-top bag. Add steak; seal and toss well to coat. Marinate in refrigerator 10 minutes.

2. While steak is marinating, cook noodles according to package directions. Drain noodles, and keep warm. Remove steak from bag, discarding marinade. Heat remaining 1 teaspoon oil in a large nonstick skillet over medium-high heat. Add green onions, and sauté 30 seconds. Add steak, and cook 4 minutes or until steak loses its pink color. Remove steak from pan, and keep warm. Add chicken broth, sugar, and tomatoes to pan, and stir well. Cover, reduce heat, and cook 3 minutes or until thick. Stir in steak, oyster sauce, and garlic, and cook 4 minutes or until thoroughly heated. Combine beef mixture with noodles in a large bowl, and toss well.

CALORIES 483; FAT 12.6g (sat 5g, mono 4.8g, poly 1.2g); PROTEIN 32.4g; CARB 54.8g; FIBER 2.2g; CHOL 57mg; IRON 4mg; SODIUM 828mg; CALC 44mg

INGREDIENT TIP

Soba noodles are protein-rich noodles native to Japan and made from a combination of buckwheat flour and wheat flour. Look for soba noodles in the ethnic or pasta section of natural food and grocery stores, or in specialty Asian markets.

Udon-Beef Noodle Bowl

This entrée falls somewhere between a soup and a noodle dish. You can eat it with chopsticks, but be sure to have spoons around to catch the broth.

Yield: 5 servings (serving size: about 1½ cups)

8 ounces uncooked udon noodles (thick, round fresh Japanese wheat noodles) or spaghetti

1½ teaspoons bottled minced garlic

½ teaspoon crushed red pepper

2 (14¼-ounce) cans lower-sodium beef broth

3 tablespoons lower-sodium soy sauce

3 tablespoons sake (rice wine) or dry sherry

1 tablespoon honey

Cooking spray

2 cups sliced shiitake mushroom caps (about 4 ounces)

½ cup thinly sliced carrot

8 ounces top round steak, thinly sliced

¾ cup diagonally cut green onions

1 (6-ounce) bag prewashed baby spinach

1. Cook noodles according to package directions; drain.
2. Place garlic, pepper, and broth in a large saucepan. Bring to a boil; reduce heat, and simmer 10 minutes.
3. Combine soy sauce, sake, and honey in a small bowl; stir with a whisk.
4. Heat a large nonstick skillet coated with cooking spray over medium-high heat. Add mushrooms and carrot; sauté 2 minutes. Stir in soy sauce mixture; cook 2 minutes, stirring constantly. Add vegetable mixture to broth mixture. Stir in beef; cook 2 minutes or until beef loses its pink color. Stir in noodles, green onions, and spinach. Serve immediately.

CALORIES 306; FAT 5.6g (sat 1.8g, mono 2g, poly 0.4g); PROTEIN 22.4g; CARB 36.6g; FIBER 2.4g; CHOL 39mg; IRON 3.4mg; SODIUM 707mg; CALC 59mg

vegetarian
dishes

Bucatini with Eggplant and Roasted Peppers

Eggplant and capers add a delectable flavor to this summery pasta sauce. If you can't find bucatini (long, hollow pasta), you can use linguine or spaghetti.

Yield: 6 servings (serving size: 1⅔ cups pasta mixture and 2 tablespoons cheese)

2 large yellow bell peppers

1 small eggplant, peeled and cut into ½-inch cubes (about ¾ pound)

1 cup water

2 tablespoons extra-virgin olive oil, divided

2 tablespoons minced fresh oregano

2 tablespoons capers

2 garlic cloves, minced

½ teaspoon salt

¼ teaspoon freshly ground black pepper

6 plum tomatoes, seeded and chopped

12 ounces uncooked bucatini or linguine

¾ cup (3 ounces) grated ricotta salata or Romano cheese

1. Preheat broiler.

2. Cut bell peppers in half lengthwise, and discard seeds and membranes. Place pepper halves, skin sides up, on a foil-lined baking sheet; flatten with hand. Broil 10 minutes or until peppers are blackened. Place in a zip-top plastic bag, and seal. Let stand 15 minutes.

3. Peel and cut bell peppers into strips. Reduce oven temperature to 425°.

4. Arrange eggplant cubes in a single layer in a 2-quart baking dish. Pour 1 cup water over eggplant. Bake at 425° for 35 minutes or until eggplant is tender, adding more water as needed.

5. Heat 1 tablespoon oil in a large nonstick skillet over medium-high heat. Add oregano, capers, and garlic; sauté 1 minute. Stir in eggplant, bell pepper strips, salt, black pepper, and tomatoes. Cover, reduce heat, and simmer 15 minutes, stirring occasionally.

6. Cook pasta according to package directions, omitting salt and fat. Drain in a colander over a bowl, reserving ½ cup cooking liquid.

7. Combine pasta, eggplant mixture, and remaining 1 tablespoon oil in a large bowl, tossing to coat. Add reserved cooking liquid, if necessary, to coat pasta. Sprinkle with cheese.

CALORIES 336; FAT 9.7g (sat 3.2g, mono 4.6g, poly 1g); PROTEIN 12.9g; CARB 50.3g; FIBER 5.7g; CHOL 15mg; IRON 2.8mg; SODIUM 461mg; CALC 182mg

MAKE AHEAD TIP

Prepare the sauce up to two days in advance, and then reheat gently over medium-low heat while you cook the pasta.

Fava Beans with Pesto and Cavatappi

Pasta is a dry ingredient that becomes water-rich when cooked. This vegetarian main dish shows off fava beans.

Yield: 8 servings (serving size: about 1¼ cups pasta and 1 tablespoon cheese)

2 pounds unshelled fava beans (about 3 cups shelled)

1 cup fresh basil leaves (about 1 ounce)

¼ cup chopped fresh mint

2 tablespoons fresh lemon juice

1 teaspoon salt

¼ teaspoon freshly ground black pepper

1 garlic clove, minced

3 tablespoons extra-virgin olive oil

1 pound uncooked cavatappi pasta

½ cup grape tomatoes, halved

½ cup (2 ounces) grated fresh Parmesan cheese

1. Remove beans from pods; discard pods. Cook beans in boiling water 1 minute. Drain and rinse with cold water; drain. Remove outer skins from beans; discard skins.

2. Combine basil and next 5 ingredients in a food processor; process until smooth. With processor on, slowly pour oil through food chute, and process until well blended.

3. Cook pasta according to package directions, omitting salt and fat; drain. Combine pasta and basil mixture in a large bowl, tossing to coat. Add beans and tomatoes, tossing to combine. Sprinkle with Parmesan cheese.

CALORIES 335; FAT 8.9g (sat 1.9g, mono 4.7g, poly 1.5g); PROTEIN 17.3g; CARB 51.9g; FIBER 2.7g; CHOL 46mg; IRON 4.1mg; SODIUM 411mg; CALC 116mg

INGREDIENT TIP

If you can't find fava beans, substitute fresh lima beans or even thawed frozen edamame.

Asian Noodle, Tofu, and Vegetable Stir-Fry

Stir-fries feel so easy and undemanding. This one is even more so because it has cellophane noodles right in it, making it a one-dish meal. Soaked dried mushrooms add flavor to the stock.

Yield: 4 servings (serving size: 2 cups)

2 ounces uncooked bean threads (cellophane noodles)

½ ounce dried wood ear mushrooms (about 6)

1 cup boiling water

2 teaspoons peanut oil or vegetable oil

1 cup coarsely chopped onion

1 tablespoon minced seeded jalapeño pepper

2 teaspoons minced peeled fresh ginger

2 garlic cloves, minced

3 cups (¼-inch) diagonally sliced carrot (about 1 pound)

¼ teaspoon salt

7 cups (1-inch) sliced bok choy

2 tablespoons lower-sodium soy sauce

1 (12.3-ounce) package reduced-fat firm tofu, cubed

3 tablespoons water

2 teaspoons cornstarch

1 teaspoon dark sesame oil or chili oil

1. Place noodles in a large bowl; cover with warm water. Let stand 20 minutes. Drain; set aside.

2. Combine mushrooms and 1 cup boiling water in a bowl; let stand 20 minutes. Strain through a sieve into a bowl, reserving mushroom liquid. Cut mushrooms into strips.

3. Heat peanut oil in a wok or nonstick Dutch oven over medium-high heat. Add onion, jalapeño, ginger, and garlic; stir-fry 1 minute. Add mushrooms, carrot, and salt; stir-fry 2 minutes. Stir in ¼ cup reserved mushroom liquid; cover and cook 3 minutes or until carrots are crisp-tender and liquid evaporates.

4. Add bok choy; stir-fry 1 minute. Stir in noodles, remaining mushroom liquid, soy sauce, and tofu; cook 2 minutes.

5. Combine 3 tablespoons water and cornstarch; pour into pan. Bring to a boil; cook 2 minutes or until slightly thick. Drizzle with sesame oil.

CALORIES 195; FAT 6.4g (sat 1g, mono 1.9g, poly 2.8g); PROTEIN 10.3g; CARB 27.4g; FIBER 6.1g; CHOL 0mg; IRON 2.6mg; SODIUM 539mg; CALC 206mg

Roasted Vegetable Pasta

This aromatic, colorful, delicious pasta will please your senses of smell, sight, and taste. You'll hardly be able to wait to sit down and eat!

Yield: 4 servings (serving size: 1½ cups pasta and 1 tablespoon cheese)

3 cups (8 ounces) uncooked farfalle (bow tie pasta)

2 cups Roasted Vegetables

1 cup frozen petite green peas, thawed

¼ cup chopped fresh parsley

¼ cup (1½ ounces) thinly shaved fresh Parmesan cheese

1. Cook pasta according to package directions, omitting salt and fat. Drain and keep warm.

2. Combine pasta, Roasted Vegetables, and peas in a large bowl. Top with parsley and cheese.

CALORIES 338; FAT 6g (sat 1.8g, mono 2.5g, poly 0.7g); PROTEIN 14.3g; CARB 54.9g; FIBER 5.5g; CHOL 5mg; IRON 3mg; SODIUM 485mg; CALC 106mg

Roasted Vegetables

Yield: 2 cups (serving size: ½ cup)

1 (8-ounce) package baby portobello mushrooms, halved

2 cups grape or cherry tomatoes

1 red onion, sliced

1 tablespoon olive oil

½ teaspoon salt

¼ teaspoon freshly ground black pepper

¼ cup dry white wine

1. Preheat oven to 475°.

2. Combine first 6 ingredients in a bowl; toss well to coat. Arrange mushroom mixture in a single layer on a jelly-roll pan.

3. Bake at 475° for 15 minutes; turn vegetables over. Drizzle wine evenly over vegetables; bake an additional 7 minutes or until vegetables are tender and lightly browned.

CALORIES 84; FAT 3.9g (sat 0.6g, mono 2.5g, poly 0.7g); PROTEIN 2.4g; CARB 9.3g; FIBER 2.2g; CHOL 0mg; IRON 0.8mg; SODIUM 302mg; CALC 15mg

Baked Goat Cheese and Roasted Winter Squash over Garlicky Fettuccine

The goat cheese rounds are baked at a high temperature to crisp the breadcrumb coating and heat the cheese just enough to melt when you cut into one.

Yield: 8 servings

6 cups (1-inch) cubed peeled kabocha or butternut squash (about 2¼ pounds)

1 large red bell pepper, cut into 1-inch pieces

1½ tablespoons olive oil, divided

Cooking spray

1 teaspoon salt, divided

1 teaspoon chopped fresh or ¼ teaspoon dried rosemary

¼ teaspoon freshly ground black pepper

2 (4-ounce) packages goat cheese

½ cup dry breadcrumbs

1 pound uncooked fettuccine

¼ teaspoon crushed red pepper

2 garlic cloves, minced

Rosemary sprigs (optional)

1. Preheat oven to 425°.

2. Place squash and bell pepper in a large bowl. Add 1 tablespoon oil; toss well. Arrange vegetables in a single layer on a jelly-roll pan coated with cooking spray. Sprinkle with ½ teaspoon salt, rosemary, and black pepper. Bake at 425° for 40 minutes, stirring once.

3. Place goat cheese in freezer 10 minutes. Cut cheese crosswise into 8 equal rounds. Place breadcrumbs in a shallow bowl. Dredge each round in breadcrumbs; place on a baking sheet. Bake at 425° for 6 minutes.

4. Cook pasta according to package directions, omitting salt and fat. Drain, reserving ½ cup cooking liquid. Return pasta to pan; add reserved cooking liquid, remaining 1½ teaspoons oil, remaining ½ teaspoon salt, red pepper, and garlic, tossing to coat. Place 1¼ cups pasta in each of 8 shallow bowls; top each serving with about ½ cup squash mixture and 1 goat cheese round. Garnish with rosemary sprigs, if desired.

CALORIES 423; FAT 14.1g (sat 7.4g, mono 4.2g, poly 0.7g); PROTEIN 17.8g; CARB 54.7g; FIBER 2.7g; CHOL 30mg; IRON 2.1mg; SODIUM 439mg; CALC 290mg

Gorgonzola-Walnut Fettuccine with Toasted Breadcrumbs

Toasted walnuts and crumbled Gorgonzola cheese enhance this easy weeknight recipe.

Yield: 4 servings (serving size: 1½ cups)

1 slice day-old hearty white bread (such as Pepperidge Farm), torn

1 tablespoon olive oil

4 garlic cloves, minced

8 ounces uncooked fettuccine

¼ cup chopped fresh parsley

¼ cup (1 ounce) crumbled Gorgonzola cheese

3 tablespoons chopped walnuts, toasted

2 teaspoons fresh lemon juice

½ teaspoon salt

¼ teaspoon freshly ground black pepper

1. Preheat oven to 250°.

2. Place bread in a food processor; pulse 10 times or until coarse crumbs measure ⅔ cup. Place breadcrumbs on a baking sheet. Bake at 250° for 30 minutes or until dry.

3. Heat olive oil in a large nonstick skillet over medium heat. Add minced garlic, and cook 30 seconds, stirring constantly. Remove garlic mixture from heat, and let stand 5 minutes. Return pan to heat. Stir in breadcrumbs; cook 6 minutes or until lightly browned, stirring mixture frequently.

4. Cook fettuccine according to package directions, omitting salt and fat; drain. Place fettuccine in a large bowl. Add breadcrumb mixture, parsley, Gorgonzola, walnuts, lemon juice, salt, and black pepper; toss gently to combine. Serve immediately.

CALORIES 327; FAT 10.4g (sat 2.5g, mono 3g, poly 3g); PROTEIN 11.1g; CARB 49.5g; FIBER 2.9g; CHOL 6.3mg; IRON 2.5mg; SODIUM 444mg; CALC 70mg

Italian Vegetable Pie

Even meat eaters are going to love this easy weeknight dish. Although vegetarian, it has a really meaty flavor.

Yield: 8 servings

2 teaspoons olive oil

1 cup chopped green bell pepper

1 cup chopped onion

1 cup chopped mushrooms

1 (12.3-ounce) package firm tofu, drained and crumbled

3 garlic cloves, minced

3 tablespoons tomato paste

1 teaspoon dried Italian seasoning

1 teaspoon fennel seeds

¼ teaspoon crushed red pepper

1 (25.5-ounce) jar fat-free marinara sauce

6 cooked lasagna noodles, cut in half crosswise

Cooking spray

1½ cups (6 ounces) shredded part-skim mozzarella cheese

¼ cup grated Parmesan cheese

1. Preheat oven to 375°.

2. Heat oil in a large nonstick skillet over medium-high heat. Add bell pepper, chopped onion, mushrooms, tofu, and garlic; sauté 3 minutes or until vegetables are tender. Stir in tomato paste, Italian seasoning, fennel seeds, crushed red pepper, and marinara sauce; bring to a boil. Reduce heat; simmer 10 minutes.

3. Arrange noodles spokelike in bottom of an 8-inch round baking dish coated with cooking spray. Spread 3 cups tomato mixture over noodles. Fold ends of noodles over tomato mixture, and top with remaining tomato mixture and cheeses. Bake at 375° for 20 minutes.

CALORIES 307; FAT 10.4g (sat 4.4g, mono 3g, poly 2.1g); PROTEIN 19.7g; CARB 33.8g; FIBER 4.8g; CHOL 20mg; IRON 6.7mg; SODIUM 444mg; CALC 340mg

INGREDIENT TIP

When a recipe calls for a small amount of tomato paste, it's convenient to use paste from a tube rather than a can. However, if you prefer canned, consider this: Spoon remaining paste by the tablespoon onto a baking sheet and freeze. Store frozen cubes in a freezer bag.

Colorful Vegetable Lasagna

Arrange the noodles crosswise in the pan to allow space for them to expand in the casserole's liquid. Serve with a salad.

Yield: 8 servings (serving size: 1 piece)

Cooking spray

1 cup chopped red bell pepper (about 1 medium)

1 cup chopped yellow bell pepper (about 1 medium)

1 cup chopped onion

4 medium zucchini, halved lengthwise and thinly sliced (about 5 cups)

2 (8-ounce) packages presliced cremini mushrooms

3 garlic cloves, minced

2 cups (8 ounces) shredded part-skim mozzarella cheese, divided

1½ cups fat-free ricotta cheese

½ cup (2 ounces) grated fresh Parmesan cheese, divided

1 large egg

5 cups Basic Marinara (recipe on page 239), divided

12 precooked lasagna noodles (about 8 ounces)

1. Preheat oven to 350°.

2. Heat a large Dutch oven over medium-high heat. Coat pan with cooking spray. Add bell peppers, onion, zucchini, and mushrooms; sauté 10 minutes or until vegetables are crisp-tender and mushroom liquid evaporates. Add garlic; sauté 30 seconds.

3. Combine 1½ cups mozzarella, ricotta, ¼ cup Parmesan, and egg, stirring well.

4. Spread 1 cup Basic Marinara over bottom of a 13 x 9–inch baking dish coated with cooking spray; top with 3 noodles. Spoon 1 cup Basic Marinara evenly over noodles. Top evenly with one-third of ricotta mixture and one-third of vegetable mixture. Repeat layers twice, ending with noodles. Top with remaining 1 cup Basic Marinara. Sprinkle evenly with remaining ½ cup mozzarella and remaining ¼ cup Parmesan. Cover and bake at 350° for 45 minutes. Uncover and bake an additional 10 minutes or until cheeses melt. Let stand 10 minutes.

CALORIES 378; FAT 11.4g (sat 5.4g, mono 4g, poly 1g); PROTEIN 22.9g; CARB 46.5g; FIBER 5.9g; CHOL 55mg; IRON 2.6mg; SODIUM 667mg; CALC 434mg

Pasta with Sun-Dried Tomato Pesto and Feta Cheese

Pasta with Sun-Dried Tomato Pesto and Feta Cheese is a spring-inspired dish that can be served year-round. The oil in the sun-dried tomatoes gives the almond-spiced pesto a rich consistency.

Yield: 4 servings (serving size: 1 cup)

1 (9-ounce) package refrigerated fresh linguine

¾ cup oil-packed sun-dried tomato halves, drained

¼ cup loosely packed basil leaves

2 tablespoons slivered almonds

2 tablespoons preshredded fresh Parmesan cheese

1 tablespoon bottled minced garlic

½ teaspoon salt

¼ teaspoon black pepper

½ cup (2 ounces) crumbled feta cheese

1. Cook pasta according to package directions, omitting salt and fat. Drain through a sieve over a bowl, reserving 1 cup cooking liquid. Return pasta to pan.

2. While pasta cooks, place tomatoes and next 6 ingredients in a food processor; process until finely chopped.

3. Combine tomato mixture and reserved 1 cup cooking liquid, stirring with a whisk.

4. Add tomato mixture to pasta; toss well to coat. Sprinkle with feta.

CALORIES 300; FAT 9.9g (sat 3.3g, mono 3.9g, poly 1.6g); PROTEIN 12.3g; CARB 42g; FIBER 4.3g; CHOL 61mg; IRON 3.1mg; SODIUM 570mg; CALC 141mg

QUICK TIP

Bottled minced garlic is a convenient, quick way to get all the flavor of garlic without all the fuss.

Lo Mein with Tofu

Although lo mein is traditionally made with Chinese egg noodles, here we substitute whole-wheat linguine. Pan-frying the tofu gives it a crisp exterior.

Yield: 4 servings (serving size: 1¾ cups)

1 (14-ounce) package firm water-packed tofu, drained and cut crosswise into 4 (1-inch-thick) pieces

8 ounces uncooked whole-wheat linguine

1 teaspoon dark sesame oil

½ teaspoon salt, divided

¼ teaspoon freshly ground black pepper, divided

2 tablespoons canola oil, divided

3 tablespoons oyster sauce

1½ tablespoons mirin (sweet rice wine)

1½ tablespoons lower-sodium soy sauce

1 teaspoon rice vinegar

¾ cup vertically sliced onion

2 cups shredded cabbage

2 cups peeled, thinly diagonally sliced carrot

2 large garlic cloves, thinly sliced

1½ cups fresh bean sprouts

¼ cup chopped green onions

1. Place tofu in a single layer on several layers of paper towels. Cover tofu with several more layers of paper towels, and top with a cast-iron skillet or other heavy pan. Let stand 30 minutes. Discard paper towels.

2. Cook pasta in boiling water until al dente; drain. Combine pasta, sesame oil, ¼ teaspoon salt, and ⅛ teaspoon pepper; toss. Set aside.

3. Sprinkle remaining ¼ teaspoon salt and remaining ⅛ teaspoon pepper evenly over tofu. Heat a large cast-iron skillet over medium-high heat. Add 1 tablespoon canola oil to pan; swirl to coat. Add tofu to pan; cook 4 minutes on each side or until golden. Remove from pan; cut into bite-sized pieces. Combine oyster sauce and next 3 ingredients in a small bowl, stirring well.

4. Heat a wok or cast-iron skillet over medium-high heat. Add remaining 1 tablespoon canola oil to pan; swirl to coat. Add onion; stir-fry 2 minutes or until lightly browned. Add cabbage, carrot, and garlic; stir-fry 2 minutes or until cabbage wilts. Reduce heat to medium; stir in tofu and vinegar mixture, tossing to coat. Add pasta and bean sprouts; toss. Cook 2 minutes or until thoroughly heated. Sprinkle with green onions.

CALORIES 397; FAT 15.4g (sat 1.3g, mono 8.8g, poly 4.1g); PROTEIN 18.2g; CARB 55.1g; FIBER 9g; CHOL 0mg; IRON 4mg; SODIUM 736mg; CALC 248mg

Easy Meatless Manicotti

This dish comes together quickly because you don't have to cook the manicotti shells.

Yield: 7 servings (serving size: 2 stuffed manicotti)

2 cups (8 ounces) shredded part-skim mozzarella cheese, divided

1 (16-ounce) carton fat-free cottage cheese

1 (10-ounce) package frozen chopped spinach, thawed, drained, and squeezed dry

¼ cup (1 ounce) grated fresh Parmesan cheese

1½ teaspoons dried oregano

¼ teaspoon salt

¼ teaspoon black pepper

1 (8-ounce) package manicotti (14 shells)

1 (26-ounce) jar fat-free tomato-basil pasta sauce

Cooking spray

1 cup water

1. Preheat oven to 375°.

2. Combine 1½ cups mozzarella, cottage cheese, and next 5 ingredients in a medium bowl. Spoon about 3 tablespoons cheese mixture into each uncooked manicotti. Pour half of tomato-basil pasta sauce into a 13 x 9–inch baking dish coated with cooking spray. Arrange stuffed shells in a single layer over sauce, and top with remaining sauce. Pour 1 cup water into dish. Sprinkle remaining ½ cup mozzarella evenly over sauce. Cover tightly with foil. Bake at 375° for 1 hour or until shells are tender. Let stand 10 minutes before serving.

CALORIES 328; FAT 9g (sat 4.8g, mono 2.2g, poly 0.5g); PROTEIN 23.8g; CARB 38.3g; FIBER 3.9g; CHOL 23mg; IRON 3mg; SODIUM 891mg; CALC 451mg

Pasta with White Beans, Greens, and Lemon

This easy dish is comforting for weeknights or a casual dinner with friends.

Yield: 6 servings

1 pound uncooked orecchiette pasta ("little ears" pasta)

2 tablespoons extra-virgin olive oil

Cooking spray

3 garlic cloves, minced

¾ cup chopped sun-dried tomatoes, packed without oil

¼ teaspoon crushed red pepper

1 (15-ounce) can cannellini beans, rinsed and drained

3 cups trimmed arugula or baby spinach

1 cup fresh basil leaves, coarsely chopped (about 1 [1-ounce] package)

1 tablespoon grated lemon rind

3 tablespoons fresh lemon juice

1 teaspoon kosher salt

5 tablespoons pine nuts, toasted

¼ cup (1 ounce) grated fresh Parmesan cheese

1. Cook pasta according to package directions, omitting salt and fat. Drain. Place pasta in a large bowl; drizzle with oil, tossing to coat.

2. Heat a large Dutch oven over medium-high heat. Coat pan with cooking spray. Add garlic to pan; sauté 1 minute or until garlic begins to brown. Add pasta mixture, tomatoes, pepper, and beans; cook 2 minutes, stirring constantly. Stir in arugula, basil, rind, juice, and salt; cook 1 minute or until arugula wilts. Spoon 1½ cups pasta mixture into each of 6 shallow bowls or plates; top each serving with 2½ teaspoons pine nuts and 2 teaspoons cheese. Serve immediately.

CALORIES 438; FAT 12.2g (sat 2g, mono 4.7g, poly 3.2g); PROTEIN 16.2g; CARB 68.2g; FIBER 5.5g; CHOL 3mg; IRON 4.4mg; SODIUM 623mg; CALC 132mg

Orecchiette with Fresh Fava Beans, Ricotta, and Shredded Mint

While fava beans are best, frozen lima beans or green peas can be used in a pinch. If using frozen beans or peas, just toss them into the pasta water during the last minute of cooking, and drain with the pasta. If you can't find orecchiette, use seashell pasta.

Yield: 6 servings (serving size: about 1 cup)

2 pounds unshelled fava beans (about 1 cup shelled)

1 pound uncooked orecchiette pasta ("little ears" pasta)

1 teaspoon extra-virgin olive oil

¾ teaspoon salt

1 cup part-skim ricotta cheese

½ cup (2 ounces) grated fresh Parmesan cheese

½ cup coarsely chopped fresh mint

½ teaspoon freshly ground black pepper

Mint sprigs (optional)

1. Remove beans from pods; discard pods. Cook beans in boiling water 1 minute. Remove beans with a slotted spoon. Plunge beans into ice water; drain. Remove tough outer skins from beans; discard skins. Set beans aside.

2. Cook pasta according to package directions, omitting salt and fat. Drain pasta, reserving 1 cup cooking liquid. Place pasta in a large bowl; add oil and salt. Toss well.

3. Combine 1 cup reserved cooking liquid, ricotta cheese, Parmesan cheese, chopped mint, and pepper. Add beans and cheese mixture to pasta mixture; toss to combine. Garnish with mint sprigs, if desired.

CALORIES 507; FAT 8.8g (sat 4.1g, mono 2.5g, poly 1.3g); PROTEIN 29.2g; CARB 85.5g; FIBER 4.7g; CHOL 25mg; IRON 6.2mg; SODIUM 540mg; CALC 255mg

INGREDIENT TIP

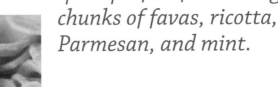

Orecchiette plumps up to nearly twice its size once cooked, and its shape is perfect for holding chunks of favas, ricotta, Parmesan, and mint.

Pasta with Asparagus and Mushrooms

If you're looking for a simple, light meal, this is it. It's super easy, and the mushrooms smell sublime while they're cooking.

Yield: 4 servings

¼ cup chopped fresh parsley

2 teaspoons chopped fresh basil

2 garlic cloves, minced

4 teaspoons butter or stick margarine

⅓ cup diced shallots

6 cups sliced cremini mushrooms

½ teaspoon salt

½ cup dry white wine

8 ounces uncooked pappardelle (wide ribbon pasta) or fettuccine

2 cups (2-inch) sliced asparagus (1 pound)

½ cup (2 ounces) grated fresh Parmesan cheese, divided

¼ teaspoon freshly ground black pepper

1. Combine first 3 ingredients, and set aside.

2. Melt butter in a large nonstick skillet over medium-high heat. Add shallots; sauté 1 minute. Add mushrooms and salt; sauté 5 minutes. Stir in wine; cook 1 minute. Reduce heat to low. Add 2 tablespoons parsley mixture; sauté 2 minutes. Keep warm.

3. Bring water to a boil in a large Dutch oven. Add pasta; cook 6½ minutes. Add asparagus; cook 1½ minutes or until asparagus is crisp-tender. Drain pasta mixture in a colander over a bowl, reserving ½ cup cooking liquid. Combine reserved cooking liquid, pasta mixture, mushroom mixture, and ¼ cup cheese. Arrange 2 cups pasta mixture on each of 4 plates. Sprinkle evenly with remaining parsley mixture, remaining ¼ cup cheese, and ¼ teaspoon pepper.

CALORIES 357; FAT 9g (sat 5g, mono 2.3g, poly 0.9g); PROTEIN 16.7g; CARB 54.2g; FIBER 4.4g; CHOL 20mg; IRON 4.8mg; SODIUM 575mg; CALC 215mg

FLAVOR TIP

For an extra-tasty touch, drizzle a few drops of truffle oil over the dish.

Homemade Pappardelle Pasta with Mushrooms, Green Peas, and Asparagus

Yield: 5 servings (serving size: 1 cup pasta and about 1½ tablespoons cheese)

Pasta:

1 teaspoon saffron threads

¼ cup water

9 ounces all-purpose flour (about 2 cups), divided

1 teaspoon salt

1 tablespoon olive oil

2 large eggs, lightly beaten

Mushroom Broth:

1 tablespoon butter

½ cup dried porcini mushrooms

8 shiitake mushroom stems

6 thyme sprigs

1 carrot, quartered

1 celery stalk, quartered

1 small onion, quartered

1 garlic clove

1 bay leaf

1 cup fat-free, lower-sodium chicken broth or vegetable broth

Remaining Ingredients:

1 tablespoon olive oil

1 tablespoon diced shallots

8 large shiitake mushroom caps, quartered

1 garlic clove, minced

½ cup (1-inch) sliced asparagus

½ cup fresh or frozen petite green peas

1 tablespoon chopped fresh chives

½ teaspoon butter

½ cup (2 ounces) grated fresh Parmesan cheese

1. To prepare pasta, combine saffron and ¼ cup water in a saucepan. Cook over low heat 10 minutes; cool. Weigh or lightly spoon flour into dry measuring cups; level with a knife. Combine 1½ cups flour and salt in a bowl. Make a well in center of mixture; add 3 tablespoons saffron water, 1 tablespoon oil, and eggs. Stir to form a dough. Turn dough out onto a lightly floured surface; shape into a ball. Knead until smooth and elastic (about 10 to 15 minutes); add remaining flour, 1 tablespoon at a time, to prevent dough from sticking to hands. Dust dough lightly with flour, and wrap in plastic wrap. Chill 1 hour.

2. Divide dough in half. Working with 1 portion at a time, pass dough through smooth rollers of a pasta machine on widest setting (cover remaining dough to keep from drying). Continue moving width gauge to narrower settings; pass dough through rollers once at each setting, dusting with flour, if needed. Repeat procedure with remaining half of dough. Cut pasta sheets into 8 x 1–inch strips. Hang pasta on a wooden drying rack (no longer than 30 minutes).

3. To prepare mushroom broth, melt 1 tablespoon butter in a saucepan over medium heat.

4. Add porcinis and next 7 ingredients; cook 5 minutes. Add broth; bring to a boil. Reduce heat to medium-low; simmer until reduced to 1¼ cups (about 25 minutes). Strain broth through a sieve into a bowl; reserve ¾ cup broth. Discard solids.

5. Cook pasta in boiling water 2 minutes or until al dente; drain.

6. Heat 1 tablespoon oil in a nonstick skillet over medium-high heat. Add shallots, mushroom caps, and minced garlic; cook 3 minutes. Add reserved ¾ cup broth; reduce heat to medium, and cook 3 minutes. Stir in asparagus, peas, chives, and ½ teaspoon butter. Add cooked pasta; toss to coat. Sprinkle with cheese.

CALORIES 346; FAT 13g (sat 4.5g, mono 6.2g, poly 1.1g); PROTEIN 13.9g; CARB 42.8g; FIBER 2.5g; CHOL 101mg; IRON 3.3mg; SODIUM 810mg; CALC 162mg

FLAVOR TIP

Don't be tempted to use more garlic in this dish; it will overpower the other flavors.

Pappardelle with Lemon, Baby Artichokes, and Asparagus

Pappardelle is a wide, flat pasta. If you can't find it, use fettuccine. Be sure to grate the rind before you juice the lemon.

Yield: 6 servings

12 ounces uncooked pappardelle
(wide ribbon pasta)

2¼ cups cold water, divided

¼ cup fresh lemon juice
(about 2 lemons)

24 baby artichokes (about 2 pounds)

3 tablespoons extra-virgin olive oil,
divided

1 pound asparagus, trimmed and
cut diagonally into 1-inch pieces

2 tablespoons chopped fresh
flat-leaf parsley

1 tablespoon grated lemon rind

1 teaspoon chopped fresh thyme

½ teaspoon salt

½ teaspoon black pepper

1¼ cups (5 ounces) grated fresh
Parmigiano-Reggiano cheese

1. Cook pasta according to package directions, omitting salt and fat. Drain pasta, reserving ½ cup cooking liquid. Set pasta aside; keep warm.

2. Combine 2 cups water and juice in a medium bowl. Working with 1 artichoke at a time, cut off stem to within ¼ inch of base; peel stem. Remove bottom leaves and tough outer leaves, leaving tender heart and bottom; trim about 1 inch from top of artichoke. Cut each artichoke in half lengthwise. Place artichoke halves in lemon water.

3. Heat 1 tablespoon oil in a large skillet over medium heat. Drain artichokes well; pat dry. Add artichokes to pan. Cover and cook 8 minutes, stirring occasionally; uncover. Increase heat to medium-high; cook 2 minutes or until artichokes are golden, stirring frequently. Place artichokes in a large bowl.

4. Place pan over medium heat; add remaining ¼ cup water and asparagus to pan. Cover and cook 5 minutes or until crisp-tender. Add asparagus, parsley, and rind to artichokes; toss well. Add pasta, reserved cooking liquid, remaining 2 tablespoons oil, thyme, salt, and pepper to artichoke mixture; toss well. Place 2 cups pasta mixture into each of 6 shallow bowls; top each serving with about 3 tablespoons cheese.

CALORIES 411; FAT 12.6g (sat 4g, mono 6.4g, poly 1.3g); PROTEIN 20.2g; CARB 59.5g; FIBER 12.2g; CHOL 15mg; IRON 3.9mg; SODIUM 644mg; CALC 217mg

Butternut Squash and Parsnip Baked Pasta

This warming, spicy, and very satisfying meatless dish combines two autumn vegetables—butternut squash and parsnips. It's homey enough to serve on weeknights and festive enough to serve during the holidays.

Yield: 4 servings (serving size: 2 cups)

1 tablespoon olive oil

1 cup finely chopped onion

¼ teaspoon crushed red pepper

2 garlic cloves, minced

2 cups (½-inch) cubed peeled butternut squash

1 cup chopped parsnip

1 tablespoon chopped fresh or 1 teaspoon dried rubbed sage

1 tablespoon chopped fresh or 1 teaspoon dried parsley

¼ teaspoon ground nutmeg

¼ teaspoon ground allspice

½ teaspoon salt, divided

½ teaspoon black pepper, divided

2 cups uncooked penne (tube-shaped pasta)

½ cup (2 ounces) grated fresh Parmesan cheese, divided

Cooking spray

1½ tablespoons butter

2 tablespoons all-purpose flour

1 cup 1% low-fat milk

Sage leaves (optional)

1. Preheat oven to 375°.

2. Heat oil in a large nonstick skillet over medium-high heat. Add onion, red pepper, and garlic; sauté 3 minutes. Add squash and parsnip; sauté 10 minutes. Stir in sage, parsley, nutmeg, allspice, ¼ teaspoon salt, and ¼ teaspoon black pepper; remove from heat.

3. Cook pasta according to package directions, omitting salt and fat. Drain in a colander over a bowl, reserving 1 cup cooking liquid. Combine squash mixture, pasta, and ¼ cup cheese in an 11 x 7–inch baking dish coated with cooking spray, tossing gently to combine.

4. Melt butter in a medium saucepan over medium heat. Add flour; cook 3 minutes, stirring constantly with a whisk. Add milk; cook 5 minutes, stirring constantly with a whisk. Gradually add reserved cooking liquid; cook 2 minutes or until thick, stirring constantly with a whisk. Add remaining ¼ teaspoon salt and remaining ¼ teaspoon pepper.

5. Pour milk mixture over pasta mixture; sprinkle with remaining ¼ cup cheese. Bake at 375° for 30 minutes or until lightly browned. Garnish with sage leaves, if desired.

CALORIES 437; FAT 13.4g (sat 6.1g, mono 5.1g, poly 1g); PROTEIN 16.5g; CARB 63.6g; FIBER 5.3g; CHOL 25mg; IRON 3.1mg; SODIUM 607mg; CALC 297mg

Fontina and Mascarpone Baked Pasta

The nutty flavor of fontina and creaminess of mascarpone create a delicious updated version of mac and cheese. For a dinner party, bake the pasta in individual gratin dishes for 15 minutes.

Yield: 8 servings (serving size: 1¼ cups)

1 pound uncooked penne (tube-shaped pasta)

1.1 ounces all-purpose flour (about ¼ cup)

3 cups fat-free milk

2 cups (8 ounces) shredded fontina cheese

¼ cup (2 ounces) mascarpone cheese

¾ teaspoon salt

¼ teaspoon freshly ground black pepper

Cooking spray

3 (1-ounce) slices white bread

1 tablespoon butter

1 small garlic clove, minced

1½ tablespoons chopped fresh parsley

1. Cook pasta according to package directions, omitting salt and fat. Drain; keep warm.

2. Preheat oven to 350°.

3. Weigh or lightly spoon flour into a dry measuring cup; level with a knife. Combine flour and milk in a large saucepan over medium heat, stirring with a whisk. Cook 10 minutes or until thick, stirring constantly with a whisk. Remove from heat; add cheeses, stirring with a whisk until smooth. Stir in salt and black pepper. Add cooked pasta, stirring to coat. Spoon pasta mixture into a 13 x 9–inch baking dish coated with cooking spray.

4. Tear bread into several pieces. Place bread in a food processor; process until fine crumbs measure 1½ cups.

5. Melt butter in a small skillet over medium heat. Add garlic; cook 30 seconds. Remove from heat. Stir in breadcrumbs until well combined. Sprinkle bread-crumb mixture evenly over pasta mixture. Bake at 350° for 25 minutes or until bubbly. Sprinkle with parsley.

CALORIES 423; FAT 14.3g (sat 8.2g, mono 3.7g, poly 0.7g); PROTEIN 19.3g; CARB 54.6g; FIBER 2.1g; CHOL 46mg; IRON 2.4mg; SODIUM 550mg; CALC 298mg

INGREDIENT TIP

If your supermarket doesn't stock mascarpone cheese, substitute full-fat cream cheese.

Vegetarian Bolognese with Whole-Wheat Penne

The Parmigiano-Reggiano rind simmers with the sauce, infusing it with deep, savory umami taste.

Yield: 6 servings

¼ cup dried porcini mushrooms (about ¼ ounce)

1 tablespoon olive oil

1½ cups finely chopped onion

½ cup finely chopped carrot

½ cup finely chopped celery

1 (8-ounce) package cremini mushrooms, finely chopped

½ cup dry red wine

¼ cup warm water

½ teaspoon salt

½ teaspoon freshly ground black pepper

1 (28-ounce) can organic crushed tomatoes with basil, undrained

1 (2-inch) piece Parmigiano-Reggiano cheese rind

12 ounces uncooked whole-wheat penne (tube-shaped pasta)

½ cup (2 ounces) shaved Parmigiano-Reggiano cheese

1. Place dried mushrooms in a spice or coffee grinder; process until finely ground.

2. Heat oil in a large saucepan over medium-high heat. Add onion, carrot, celery, and cremini mushrooms; sauté 10 minutes. Add wine; simmer 2 minutes or until liquid almost evaporates. Add ¼ cup warm water and next 4 ingredients to onion mixture. Stir in ground porcini. Cover, reduce heat, and simmer 40 minutes. Keep warm. Remove rind; discard.

3. Cook pasta according to package directions, omitting salt and fat. Place 1 cup pasta in each of 6 bowls. Top each portion with ¾ cup sauce and about 1 tablespoon cheese.

CALORIES 334; FAT 7.2g (sat 2.1g, mono 2.5g, poly 1.9g); PROTEIN 14.8g; CARB 57.7g; FIBER 9.7g; CHOL 9mg; IRON 3.3mg; SODIUM 542mg; CALC 156mg

Pasta with Mushrooms and Pumpkin-Gorgonzola Sauce

Any short pasta will work in this dish. For the sauce, we recommend our favorite brand of cheese: Saladena Gorgonzola; when melted into the other ingredients, it yields a luscious consistency.

Yield: 6 servings (serving size: 1½ cups)

1 pound uncooked pennette (small penne)

1 tablespoon olive oil

5 cups thinly sliced shiitake mushroom caps (about ¾ pound whole mushrooms)

4 cups vertically sliced onion

4 garlic cloves, minced

1 teaspoon chopped fresh sage

1 (12-ounce) can evaporated milk

1½ tablespoons cornstarch

1½ tablespoons cold water

½ cup (2 ounces) crumbled Gorgonzola cheese

½ cup canned pumpkin

1 teaspoon salt

½ teaspoon freshly ground black pepper

⅛ teaspoon grated whole nutmeg

Sage sprigs (optional)

1. Cook pasta according to package directions, omitting salt and fat. Keep warm.

2. Heat oil in a Dutch oven over medium-high heat. Add mushrooms, onion, and garlic; cover and cook 3 minutes. Uncover; cook 5 minutes or until tender, stirring occasionally.

3. Combine chopped sage and milk in a medium saucepan over medium heat. Bring to a simmer. Combine cornstarch and 1½ tablespoons cold water, stirring with a whisk. Add cornstarch mixture and cheese to milk mixture, stirring with a whisk. Cook 2 minutes or until thick and smooth, stirring constantly. Remove from heat; stir in pumpkin, salt, pepper, and nutmeg.

4. Add pasta and pumpkin mixture to mushroom mixture; toss well to combine. Garnish with sage sprigs, if desired.

CALORIES 462; FAT 6.5g (sat 2.8g, mono 1.7g, poly 0.4g); PROTEIN 19.9g; CARB 83.1g; FIBER 7.3g; CHOL 11mg; IRON 3.7mg; SODIUM 636mg; CALC 265mg

NUTRITION TIP

While fresh pumpkin is only available seasonally, canned pumpkin is stocked year-round at your local supermarket and offers the same nutritional value as fresh.

Pad Thai with Tofu

Forget the Thai restaurant, and eat in! This vegetarian pad thai dish is even better than take-out. It's easy to make and tastes terrific.

Yield: 5 servings (serving size: 2 cups)

Sauce:

¼ cup lower-sodium soy sauce

2 tablespoons rice vinegar

1 to 2 tablespoons hot sauce

1 tablespoon mirin (sweet rice wine)

1 tablespoon maple syrup

Noodles:

1 teaspoon vegetable oil

2 cups thinly sliced shiitake mushroom caps (about 5 ounces)

1 cup grated carrot

1 garlic clove, minced

8 ounces extra-firm tofu, drained and cut into ½-inch cubes

1 cup light coconut milk

2 cups shredded romaine lettuce

1 cup fresh bean sprouts

1 cup (1-inch) sliced green onion tops

1 cup chopped fresh cilantro

⅓ cup dry-roasted peanuts

8 ounces uncooked wide rice sticks (rice-flour noodles; banh poh) cooked and drained

5 lime wedges

1. To prepare sauce, combine first 5 ingredients, stirring with a whisk.

2. To prepare noodles, heat oil in a large nonstick skillet over medium-high heat. Add mushrooms, carrot, and garlic; sauté 2 minutes. Add sauce and tofu; cook 1 minute. Stir in coconut milk; cook 2 minutes. Stir in lettuce and next 5 ingredients; cook 1 minute. Serve with lime wedges.

CALORIES 385; FAT 12.5g (sat 3g, mono 4g, poly 4.2g); PROTEIN 13.5g; CARB 55.8g; FIBER 4.6g; CHOL 0mg; IRON 7.1mg; SODIUM 868mg; CALC 365mg

Curried Noodles with Tofu

Look for curry paste in the Asian foods section of your supermarket. Use it conservatively though—a little goes a long way.

Yield: 4 servings (serving size: 1¼ cups)

6 ounces uncooked rice sticks (rice-flour noodles), angel hair pasta, or vermicelli

1 cup light coconut milk

1 tablespoon sugar

2 tablespoons lower-sodium soy sauce

1½ tablespoons bottled ground fresh ginger (such as Spice World)

2 teaspoons bottled minced garlic

1 teaspoon green curry paste

½ teaspoon salt

Cooking spray

1 (12.3-ounce) package extra-firm tofu, drained and cut into 1-inch cubes

1 cup red bell pepper strips

4 cups shredded napa (Chinese) cabbage

1 cup chopped green onions

3 tablespoons chopped fresh cilantro

1. Place noodles in a large bowl. Add hot water to cover; let stand 5 minutes. Drain.

2. Combine coconut milk, sugar, soy sauce, ginger, garlic, curry paste, and salt in a small bowl.

3. Heat a large nonstick skillet over medium-high heat. Coat pan with cooking spray. Add tofu; sauté 10 minutes or until golden brown. Remove tofu from pan; keep warm.

4. Add bell pepper to pan; sauté 1 minute or until crisp-tender. Add cabbage; sauté 30 seconds. Stir in noodles, coconut milk mixture, and tofu; cook 2 minutes or until noodles are tender. Stir in green onions and cilantro.

CALORIES 300; FAT 4.9g (sat 2.3g, mono 0.4g, poly 1.1g); PROTEIN 11.5g; CARB 51.4g; FIBER 4.5g; CHOL 0mg; IRON 3.6mg; SODIUM 678mg; CALC 89mg

FLAVOR TIP

Coconut milk gives this meatless dish a velvety richness.

Mushroom Pasta Bake

A full cup of Italian Asiago cheese gives body and flavor to the velvety sauce, which is laced with sherry.

Yield: 4 servings

8 ounces uncooked gigli or radiatore pasta

2 teaspoons butter

¼ cup sliced shallots

8 ounces sliced shiitake mushroom caps

4 ounces sliced cremini mushrooms

1 tablespoon chopped fresh thyme

½ teaspoon salt

¼ teaspoon freshly ground black pepper

3 garlic cloves, minced

1 tablespoon dry sherry

1.1 ounces all-purpose flour (about ¼ cup)

2 cups 2% reduced-fat milk

1 cup (4 ounces) grated Asiago cheese, divided

Cooking spray

Thyme sprigs (optional)

1. Preheat oven to 375°.

2. Cook pasta according to package directions, omitting salt and fat. Drain well. Set cooked pasta aside.

3. Melt butter in a large nonstick skillet over medium-high heat. Add shallots; sauté 3 minutes. Add mushrooms, 1 tablespoon chopped thyme, salt, pepper, and garlic; sauté 8 minutes or until mushrooms are tender. Add sherry; cook 1 minute, stirring frequently. Remove from heat.

4. Weigh or lightly spoon flour into a dry measuring cup; level with a knife. Place flour in a Dutch oven over medium-high heat; gradually add milk, stirring constantly with a whisk. Bring mixture to a boil; cook 1 minute or until slightly thick, stirring constantly with a whisk. Remove from heat; add ½ cup cheese, stirring until melted. Add pasta and mushroom mixture to cheese mixture, tossing well to combine. Spoon pasta mixture into an 8-inch square baking dish lightly coated with cooking spray; sprinkle evenly with remaining ½ cup cheese. Bake at 375° for 30 minutes or until cheese melts and begins to brown. Garnish with thyme sprigs, if desired.

CALORIES 474; FAT 16g (sat 8g, mono 4.6g, poly 2.2g); PROTEIN 21.8g; CARB 61.4g; FIBER 3.3g; CHOL 40mg; IRON 3.9mg; SODIUM 745mg; CALC 386mg

Spinach-and-Cheese Ravioli with Tomato-Basil Sauce

The ravioli should be cooked as soon as possible, or the filling will soak through the wonton wrapper and get sticky.

Yield: 4 servings (serving size: 4 ravioli, ½ cup sauce, and 1 tablespoon cheese)

Ravioli:

½ cup part-skim ricotta cheese

⅓ cup (1⅓ ounces) grated fresh Romano cheese

¼ teaspoon salt

⅛ teaspoon ground nutmeg

1 (10-ounce) package frozen chopped spinach, thawed, drained, and squeezed dry

1 large egg white, lightly beaten

32 wonton wrappers

1 large egg white, lightly beaten

1 tablespoon cornstarch

Sauce:

2 teaspoons olive oil

4 garlic cloves, chopped

1 teaspoon sugar

¼ teaspoon salt

¼ teaspoon crushed red pepper

2 (14.5-ounce) cans no-salt-added diced tomatoes, drained

¼ cup chopped fresh basil

¼ cup (1 ounce) grated fresh Romano cheese

1. To prepare ravioli, combine first 6 ingredients in a bowl.

2. Working with 1 wonton wrapper at a time (cover remaining wrappers with a damp towel to keep from drying), spoon about 1 level tablespoon spinach mixture into center of each wrapper. Brush edges of wrapper with second beaten egg white, and top with another wrapper, stretching the top slightly to meet edges of bottom wrapper. Press edges together firmly with fingers. Cut ravioli into rounds with a 3-inch biscuit cutter; discard edges. Place ravioli on a large baking sheet sprinkled with cornstarch. Fill a large Dutch oven with water, and bring to a simmer; add half of ravioli (cover remaining ravioli with a damp towel to keep from drying). Cook 4 to 5 minutes or until done (do not boil). Remove ravioli with a slotted spoon. Keep warm. Repeat procedure with remaining ravioli.

3. To prepare sauce, heat oil in a saucepan over medium heat. Add garlic; sauté 1 minute. Stir in sugar, salt, pepper, and tomatoes; bring to a boil. Reduce heat, and simmer 2 minutes. Remove from heat; stir in basil. Spoon sauce over ravioli, and top with ¼ cup Romano.

CALORIES 298; FAT 9.9g (sat 4.8g, mono 3.7g, poly 0.7g); PROTEIN 17.3g; CARB 35.9g; FIBER 2.2g; CHOL 30mg; IRON 3.4mg; SODIUM 830mg; CALC 406mg

Ziti Baked with Spinach, Tomatoes, and Smoked Gouda

This satisfying meatless casserole oozes with al dente tubes of ziti, bright yellow peppers, fire-engine red diced tomatoes, tender baby spinach, and smoky shredded Gouda.

Yield: 5 servings

8 ounces uncooked ziti (short tube-shaped pasta)

1 tablespoon olive oil

1 cup chopped onion

1 cup chopped yellow bell pepper

3 garlic cloves, minced

1 (14.5-ounce) can diced tomatoes with basil, garlic, and oregano, undrained

1 (10-ounce) can Italian-seasoned diced tomatoes, undrained (such as Rotel Bold Italian)

4 cups baby spinach

1¼ cups (5 ounces) shredded smoked Gouda cheese, divided

Cooking spray

1. Preheat oven to 375°.

2. Cook pasta according to package directions, omitting salt and fat. Drain well.

3. Heat oil in a Dutch oven over medium-high heat. Add onion and bell pepper; sauté 5 minutes. Add garlic to pan; sauté 2 minutes or until onion is tender. Stir in tomatoes; bring to a boil. Reduce heat, and simmer 5 minutes, stirring occasionally. Add spinach to pan; cook 30 seconds or until spinach wilts, stirring frequently. Remove from heat. Add pasta and ¾ cup cheese to tomato mixture, tossing well to combine. Spoon pasta mixture into an 11 x 7–inch baking dish lightly coated with cooking spray; sprinkle evenly with remaining ½ cup cheese. Bake at 375° for 15 minutes or until cheese melts and begins to brown.

CALORIES 382; FAT 12.7g (sat 5.7g, mono 4.6g, poly 0.9g); PROTEIN 17g; CARB 52.3g; FIBER 4.3g; CHOL 33mg; IRON 4.4mg; SODIUM 977mg; CALC 334mg

INGREDIENT TIP

Smoked Gouda, with its edible brown rind, creamy yellow interior, and nutlike flavor, is one of America's favorite Dutch cheeses. It shreds easily, melts quickly, and can be added near the end of the cooking time.

international
noodles

Greek-Style Scampi

This quick, filling weeknight meal relies on easy-to-find ingredients. Add a spinach-mushroom salad to round out the menu.

Yield: 4 servings

6 ounces uncooked angel hair pasta

1 teaspoon olive oil

½ cup chopped green bell pepper

2 teaspoons bottled minced garlic

1 (14.5-ounce) can diced tomatoes with basil, garlic, and oregano, undrained

⅛ teaspoon black pepper

1 pound peeled and deveined medium shrimp

⅛ teaspoon ground red pepper

6 tablespoons (about 1½ ounces) crumbled feta cheese

1. Cook pasta according to package directions, omitting salt and fat. Drain and keep warm.

2. Heat oil in a large nonstick skillet over medium-high heat. Add green bell pepper to pan; sauté 1 minute. Add garlic and tomatoes; cook 1 minute. Add black pepper and shrimp; cover and cook 3 minutes or until shrimp reach desired degree of doneness. Stir in red pepper; remove from heat. Place 1 cup pasta on each of 4 plates. Top each serving with 1 cup shrimp mixture and 1½ tablespoons cheese.

CALORIES 379; FAT 8.5g (sat 3g, mono 2.8g, poly 1.7g); PROTEIN 31.7g; CARB 43.3g; FIBER 2.6g; CHOL 185mg; IRON 4.1mg; SODIUM 139mg; CALC 656mg

QUICK TIP

Prechopped bell pepper is now widely available in the produce section of most supermarkets and is a definite time-saver.

Cavatappi Niçoise

Mediterranean white tuna perfectly complements the other distinctive flavors in this delicious salad. Look for this premium product at specialty markets.

Yield: 4 servings (serving size: 2¼ cups)

8 ounces haricots verts, trimmed and halved

8 ounces uncooked cavatappi pasta

1 (7.76-ounce) can solid white tuna, packed in oil, undrained

1 cup grape tomatoes, halved

⅓ cup niçoise olives, pitted

2 tablespoons minced shallots

2 tablespoons capers, drained

2 tablespoons extra-virgin olive oil

1 tablespoon red wine vinegar

1 tablespoon balsamic vinegar

¼ teaspoon freshly ground black pepper

⅛ teaspoon salt

4 anchovy fillets, drained

1. Cook beans in boiling water 3 minutes; remove with a slotted spoon. Rinse under cold water; drain. Place beans in a large bowl. Cook pasta according to package directions, omitting salt and fat. Drain and rinse under cold water; drain. Add pasta to beans.

2. Drain tuna through a sieve over a bowl, reserving oil. Flake tuna with a fork. Add tuna and next 4 ingredients to pasta mixture; toss. Combine reserved oil, olive oil, and next 5 ingredients in a blender; process until smooth. Pour oil mixture over pasta mixture; toss to coat.

CALORIES 431; FAT 12.8g (sat 1.6g, mono 7.7g, poly 1.6g); PROTEIN 26.5g; CARB 50.4g; FIBER 3.9g; CHOL 23mg; IRON 2.8mg; SODIUM 852mg; CALC 59mg

Spicy Asian Lettuce Wraps

Lettuce wraps have become quite the rage at many restaurants, but they can be high in sodium. This homemade version uses lower-sodium soy sauce and just 2 teaspoons of flavor-packed sesame oil for a healthier dish. You can increase or decrease the chile paste to suit your taste.

Yield: 4 servings (serving size: 3 lettuce wraps)

2½ ounces bean threads (cellophane noodles)

¼ cup minced fresh cilantro

¼ cup lower-sodium soy sauce

1 tablespoon chile paste with garlic (such as sambal oelek)

2 teaspoons dark sesame oil

2 cups chopped roasted skinless, boneless chicken

12 large Boston or romaine lettuce leaves

1. Cover bean threads with boiling water. Let stand 5 minutes or until softened. Drain, and rinse under cool water. Chop noodles.

2. While bean threads soak, combine cilantro, soy sauce, chile paste, and oil in a large bowl, stirring with a whisk. Add noodles and chicken to soy sauce mixture; toss well to coat. Spoon about ⅓ cup chicken mixture down center of each lettuce leaf; roll up.

CALORIES 213; FAT 4.9g (sat 1g, mono 1.8g, poly 1.5g); PROTEIN 23.2g; CARB 18.3g; FIBER 0.7g; CHOL 60mg; IRON 1.7mg; SODIUM 641mg; CALC 31mg

INGREDIENT TIP

Translucent cellophane noodles are known by a variety of names, including bean threads,

Chinese vermicelli, glass noodles, and bai fun. Instead of boiling, just soak them briefly in boiling water to soften.

Roasted Vegetable Couscous with Chickpeas and Onion–Pine Nut Topping

Yield: 6 servings (serving size: about ¾ cup vegetables, about ⅔ cup couscous, and 2 tablespoons topping)

Couscous:

5 cups diced peeled sweet potato

2 cups (½-inch) diced peeled parsnips (about 10 ounces)

1½ tablespoons extra-virgin olive oil

1 teaspoon Ras el Hanout

3 carrots, peeled and cut crosswise into 2-inch pieces (about 9 ounces)

1 teaspoon kosher salt, divided

1¼ cups organic vegetable broth

1 cup uncooked couscous

1 (15-ounce) can no-salt-added chickpeas (garbanzo beans), rinsed and drained

Topping:

1 tablespoon olive oil

1 yellow onion, cut into ¼-inch-thick slices, separated into rings

¼ cup pine nuts

¼ cup raisins

1 teaspoon ground cinnamon

1 tablespoon honey

1. Preheat oven to 450°.

2. To prepare couscous, combine first 5 ingredients in a large bowl; stir in ½ teaspoon salt. Place potato mixture on a baking sheet. Bake at 450° for 30 minutes or until vegetables are tender, stirring occasionally.

3. Bring broth to a boil in a medium saucepan. Stir in couscous and remaining ½ teaspoon salt. Remove from heat; cover and let stand 10 minutes. Fluff with a fork; gently stir in chickpeas. Keep warm.

4. To prepare topping, heat 1 tablespoon oil in a medium skillet over medium heat. Add onion to pan; cook 12 minutes or until tender and golden brown, stirring occasionally. Add pine nuts and raisins; cook 2 minutes. Stir in cinnamon; cook 30 seconds. Stir in honey, and remove from heat.

5. Mound couscous in middle of a serving platter. Place roasted vegetables around base of couscous. Arrange 5 carrots vertically around couscous; spoon topping over top of couscous.

CALORIES 520; FAT 13.7g (sat 1.5g, mono 7.4g, poly 3.8g); PROTEIN 11.7g; CARB 90.5g; FIBER 13.9g; CHOL 0mg; IRON 3.5mg; SODIUM 688mg; CALC 135mg

Ras el Hanout

Yield: About 3½ tablespoons (serving size: 1 teaspoon)

2 teaspoons ground ginger

2 teaspoons ground coriander

1½ teaspoons ground cinnamon

1½ teaspoons freshly ground black pepper

1½ teaspoons ground turmeric

1¼ teaspoons ground nutmeg

1 teaspoon ground allspice

½ teaspoon ground cloves

1. Combine all ingredients; store in an airtight container.

CALORIES 9; FAT 0.3g (sat 0.1g, mono 0.1g, poly 0.0g); PROTEIN 0.2g; CARB 1.6g; FIBER 0.8g; CHOL 0mg; IRON 0.4mg; SODIUM 1mg; CALC 12mg

North African Chicken and Couscous

Couscous, cumin, and cilantro are common elements in North African cuisine, as is the combination of savory and sweet. This dish makes a quick weeknight meal.

Yield: 6 servings (serving size: 2 cups)

2 cups water

1½ cups uncooked couscous

½ cup golden raisins

½ cup thawed orange juice concentrate, undiluted

⅓ cup lemon juice

2 tablespoons water

2 tablespoons olive oil

2 teaspoons ground cumin

½ teaspoon salt

¼ teaspoon black pepper

3 cups chopped roasted skinless, boneless chicken breasts (about 3 breasts)

2 cups chopped peeled cucumber

1 cup chopped red bell pepper

¼ cup thinly sliced green onions

½ cup chopped fresh cilantro

Sliced green onions (optional)

1. Bring 2 cups water to a boil in a medium saucepan, and gradually stir in couscous and raisins. Remove from heat. Cover; let stand 5 minutes. Fluff with a fork.

2. Combine orange juice and next 6 ingredients; stir well with a whisk.

3. Combine couscous mixture, juice mixture, chicken, and next 4 ingredients in a large bowl, and toss well. Garnish with green onions, if desired.

CALORIES 332; FAT 6.6g (sat 1.2g, mono 3.9g, poly 0.9g); PROTEIN 19.6g; CARB 51.2g; FIBER 3.3g; CHOL 35mg; IRON 2.8mg; SODIUM 498mg; CALC 51mg

FLAVOR TIP

Fresh and dried fruits such as apricots, dates, figs, raisins, and nuts are basic foods in many

countries bordering the Mediterranean. Moist, golden raisins add a hint of sweetness to this couscous.

Fruited Israeli Couscous

The only tools this recipe requires are a saucepan, a cutting board, and a knife. Cinnamon sticks steeped in the cooking liquid lend warm spiciness to the couscous and dried fruit.

Yield: 12 servings (serving size: about ⅔ cup)

2 teaspoons butter

1 cup finely chopped onion

½ cup dried currants

½ cup diced dried apricots

½ teaspoon salt

3 (14-ounce) cans fat-free, lower-sodium chicken broth

3 (3-inch) cinnamon sticks

2½ cups uncooked Israeli couscous

¼ cup chopped fresh cilantro

1. Melt butter in a large saucepan over medium-high heat. Add onion, and sauté 5 minutes. Stir in currants, apricots, salt, broth, and cinnamon sticks; bring to a boil. Add couscous, and return to a boil. Cover, reduce heat, and simmer 15 minutes. Let couscous mixture stand 5 minutes. Discard cinnamon sticks. Stir in cilantro.

CALORIES 190; FAT 0.9g (sat 0.4g, mono 0.2g, poly 0.1g); PROTEIN 6.5g; CARB 38.2g; FIBER 2.8g; CHOL 2mg; IRON 1mg; SODIUM 297mg; CALC 21mg

INGREDIENT TIP

Israeli couscous has bead-sized grains that are much larger than those of regular couscous, and it takes just 15 minutes to cook.

Quick Bouillabaisse Pasta

Toss together a salad, and serve with slices of crusty bread for a quick, easy, and delicious meal.

Yield: 4 servings

1 (9-ounce) package refrigerated fettuccine

1 tablespoon olive oil

1 teaspoon bottled minced garlic

2 teaspoons all-purpose flour

½ teaspoon herbes de Provence

¼ teaspoon ground turmeric

1 (14.5-ounce) can diced tomatoes, undrained

1 (8-ounce) bottle clam juice

12 medium mussels, cleaned and debearded

8 ounces medium shrimp, peeled and deveined

1 (8-ounce) halibut fillet, cut into 1-inch pieces

Chopped fresh basil (optional)

1. Cook refrigerated fettuccine according to package directions, omitting salt and fat. Drain and keep warm.

2. Heat oil in large nonstick skillet over medium-high heat. Add garlic to pan; cook 1 minute. Add flour to pan; cook 30 seconds, stirring constantly with a whisk. Stir in herbes de Provence, turmeric, tomatoes, and clam juice; bring to a boil. Stir in mussels, shrimp, and fish. Cover, reduce heat, and simmer 5 minutes or until mussels open. Discard any unopened shells.

3. Place 1 cup pasta in each of 4 bowls; top each serving with about ⅓ cup fish mixture and 3 mussels. Garnish with basil, if desired.

CALORIES 407; FAT 8.3g (sat 1.2g, mono 3.5g, poly 2g); PROTEIN 37.5g; CARB 41.5g; FIBER 3.6g; CHOL 119mg; IRON 4.4mg; SODIUM 632mg; CALC 96mg

Spicy Malaysian-Style Stir-Fried Noodles

This popular Southeast Asian street fare is known as mee goreng (fried noodles). Look for the sweet bean sauce and noodles (which are sometimes frozen) at Asian markets; substitute dried linguine for lo mein. You can always use less chile paste to make a milder version.

Yield: 6 servings (serving size: 1⅔ cups)

1 (14-ounce) package water-packed extra-firm tofu, drained

1 (1-pound) package fresh Chinese lo mein egg noodles

2 tablespoons dark sesame oil

4 garlic cloves, minced

¼ teaspoon salt

4 heads baby bok choy, trimmed and cut crosswise into 2-inch-thick strips

1 tablespoon sugar

3 tablespoons chile paste with garlic (such as sambal oelek)

2 tablespoons fresh lime juice

2 tablespoons sweet bean sauce

2 tablespoons lower-sodium soy sauce

1. Line a plate with a triple layer of paper towels; top with tofu. Place a triple layer of paper towels on top of tofu; top with another plate. Let stand 20 minutes. Cut tofu into ½-inch cubes.

2. Cook noodles in a large pan of boiling water 3 minutes or until desired degree of doneness; drain in a colander over a bowl, reserving 1 cup cooking liquid. Wipe pan with paper towels. Heat oil in pan over medium heat. Add garlic to pan; cook 30 seconds, stirring constantly. Add salt and bok choy; cook 30 seconds, stirring frequently. Stir in ½ cup reserved cooking liquid; bring to a boil. Reduce heat, and cook 4 minutes.

3. Combine sugar and next 4 ingredients, stirring until combined. Add noodles, remaining ½ cup cooking liquid, and sugar mixture to pan; toss to combine. Cook 30 seconds or until thoroughly heated, tossing to coat. Add tofu; toss to combine. Serve immediately.

CALORIES 359; FAT 9.5g (sat 1.4g, mono 2.6g, poly 4.2g); PROTEIN 15.1g; CARB 53g; FIBER 2.1g; CHOL 17mg; IRON 3.4mg; SODIUM 617mg; CALC 65mg

Caramelized Pork and Rice Noodle Salad

Yield: 6 servings (serving size: 1⅔ cups salad, about 2 ounces pork, and 4 teaspoons peanuts)

Dressing:

¾ cup water

4½ tablespoons granulated sugar

3 tablespoons rice vinegar

2 tablespoons fresh lime juice

1½ tablespoons fish sauce

2 teaspoons minced peeled fresh ginger

¾ teaspoon Sriracha (hot chile sauce, such as Huy Fong)

3 garlic cloves, minced

Salad:

1 (6-ounce) package rice vermicelli

1 pound pork tenderloin, trimmed

2 teaspoons fish sauce

1 teaspoon Sriracha

¼ teaspoon garlic powder

¼ teaspoon salt

¼ teaspoon freshly ground black pepper

3 tablespoons brown sugar

Cooking spray

2 cups thinly sliced red leaf lettuce

1 cup matchstick-cut peeled English cucumber

1 cup matchstick-cut carrots

1 cup bean sprouts

¼ cup chopped fresh basil

¼ cup chopped fresh cilantro

3 tablespoons chopped fresh mint

½ cup chopped dry-roasted peanuts

Lime wedges (optional)

1. To prepare dressing, combine first 8 ingredients in a small saucepan; cook over medium heat 5 minutes or just until sugar dissolves. Remove from heat; cool.

2. To prepare salad, place vermicelli in a large bowl. Cover with boiling water. Let stand 20 minutes or until tender. Drain and rinse under cold water; drain.

3. Preheat grill.

4. Cut tenderloin in half lengthwise. Cut each piece in half crosswise. Place each pork piece between 2 sheets of plastic wrap; pound to an even thickness using a meat mallet or small heavy skillet. Combine 2 teaspoons fish sauce and 1 teaspoon Sriracha; drizzle over pork. Sprinkle evenly with garlic powder, salt, and pepper. Pat brown sugar onto pork. Place pork on grill rack coated with cooking spray. Grill 12 minutes or until slightly pink in center, turning pieces occasionally to prevent burning. Place pork on a cutting board; let stand 5 minutes. Cut across grain into very thin slices.

5. Combine vermicelli, lettuce, and next 6 ingredients in a large bowl. Pour dressing over salad; toss well. Top with pork and nuts. Serve with lime wedges, if desired.

CALORIES 342; FAT 8.3g (sat 1.9g, mono 3.7g, poly 1.9g); PROTEIN 19.9g; CARB 47.6g; FIBER 2.7g; CHOL 43mg; IRON 1.9mg; SODIUM 821mg; CALC 48mg

FLAVOR TIP

Granulated sugar in the dressing harmonizes with the savory fish sauce, acidic vinegar and lime juice, and slightly bitter fresh herbs.

Lemongrass Shrimp over Rice Vermicelli and Vegetables

Yield: 8 servings

Shrimp:

⅓ cup Thai fish sauce (such as Three Crabs)

¼ cup sugar

2 tablespoons finely chopped peeled fresh lemongrass

1 tablespoon vegetable oil

2 garlic cloves, minced

32 large shrimp, peeled and deveined (about 1½ pounds)

Sauce:

1 cup fresh lime juice (about 9 medium limes)

¾ cup shredded carrot

½ cup sugar

¼ cup Thai fish sauce

2 garlic cloves, minced

2 red Thai chiles, seeded and minced

Shallot Oil:

¼ cup vegetable oil

¾ cup thinly sliced shallots

Remaining Ingredients:

8 ounces rice vermicelli (banh hoai or bun giang tay)

3½ cups shredded Boston lettuce, divided

2 cups fresh bean sprouts, divided

1¾ cups shredded carrot, divided

1 medium cucumber, halved lengthwise, seeded, and thinly sliced (about 1½ cups), divided

Cooking spray

½ cup chopped fresh mint

½ cup finely chopped, unsalted dry-roasted peanuts

1. To prepare shrimp, combine first 6 ingredients in a large zip-top plastic bag; seal. Marinate in refrigerator 1 hour, turning occasionally. Remove shrimp from bag; discard marinade.

2. To prepare sauce, combine lime juice and next 5 ingredients, stirring with a whisk until sugar dissolves. Set aside.

3. To prepare shallot oil, heat ¼ cup oil in a small saucepan over medium heat. Add shallots; cook 5 minutes or until golden brown. Strain shallot mixture through a sieve over a bowl. Reserve oil. Set fried shallots aside.

4. To prepare remaining ingredients, place rice vermicelli in a large bowl; cover with boiling water. Let stand 20 minutes. Drain. Combine noodles, shallot oil, 1¾ cups lettuce, 1 cup sprouts, 1 cup carrot, and ¾ cup cucumber, tossing well.

5. Preheat grill to medium-high heat.

6. Place shrimp on grill rack coated with cooking spray; grill 2½ minutes on each side or until desired degree of doneness. Place ¾ cup noodle mixture in each of 8 bowls; top each serving with 4 shrimp, about 3 tablespoons sauce, and about 1 tablespoon fried shallots. Serve with remaining lettuce, bean sprouts, carrot, cucumber, mint, and peanuts.

CALORIES 423; FAT 13.5g (sat 2.1g, mono 4.1g, poly 6g); PROTEIN 26.6g; CARB 51.9g; FIBER 4.3g; CHOL 129mg; IRON 4.2mg; SODIUM 960mg; CALC 102mg

INGREDIENT TIP

You can substitute pork tenderloin, beef sirloin, or chicken for the shrimp. Simply cut the meat into cubes, marinate for two hours, and then skewer and grill until done.

Five-Spice Pork Lo Mein

Cutting the cooked noodles makes them easier to combine with the other ingredients and easier to serve, too.

Yield: 6 servings (serving size: 1⅓ cups)

8 ounces uncooked Chinese-style noodles

1 tablespoon grated peeled fresh ginger

2 teaspoons five-spice powder

1 (¾-pound) pork tenderloin, trimmed and cut into thin strips

½ teaspoon salt, divided

2 tablespoons toasted peanut oil

¼ cup water

¼ cup hoisin sauce

½ cup chopped green onions

1. Cook noodles according to package directions, omitting salt and fat; drain. Place in a large bowl. Snip noodles several times with kitchen scissors.

2. Combine ginger, five-spice powder, and pork in a medium bowl; add ¼ teaspoon salt, tossing to coat. Heat oil in a large nonstick skillet over medium-high heat. Add pork mixture; sauté 2 minutes or until browned. Stir in remaining ¼ teaspoon salt, ¼ cup water, and hoisin sauce; cook 2 minutes or until pork reaches desired degree of doneness. Add pork mixture and green onions to noodles; toss well to combine.

CALORIES 273; FAT 8.9g (sat 1.9g, mono 3.6g, poly 2g); PROTEIN 16.3g; CARB 34.8g; FIBER 5.7g; CHOL 38mg; IRON 2.8mg; SODIUM 399mg; CALC 31mg

INGREDIENT TIP

Chinese five-spice powder is a common spice blend that can be found in most supermarkets. Its five assertive components are cinnamon, cloves, fennel seed, star anise, and Szechuan peppercorns.

Cambodian Summer Rolls

The fresh herbs, sweet shrimp, slight spicy heat, and crisp lettuce offer well-balanced taste and texture.

Yield: 12 servings (serving size: 1 roll and about 1½ tablespoons sauce)

Rolls:

6 cups water

1 pound medium shrimp

6 ounces uncooked rice noodles

12 (8-inch) round sheets rice paper

¼ cup hoisin sauce

3 cups shredded red leaf lettuce

¼ cup thinly sliced fresh basil

¼ cup thinly sliced fresh mint

Dipping Sauce:

⅓ cup lower-sodium soy sauce

¼ cup water

2 tablespoons sugar

2 tablespoons chopped fresh cilantro

2 tablespoons fresh lime juice

1 teaspoon minced peeled fresh ginger

1 teaspoon chile paste with garlic (such as sambal oelek)

1 garlic clove, minced

1. To prepare rolls, bring 6 cups water to a boil in a large saucepan. Add shrimp; cook 3 minutes or until desired degree of doneness. Drain and rinse with cold water. Peel shrimp; chill.

2. Place rice noodles in a large bowl; cover with boiling water. Let stand 8 minutes; drain.

3. Add cold water to a large, shallow dish to a depth of 1 inch. Place 1 rice paper sheet in water. Let stand 2 minutes or until soft. Place rice paper sheet on a flat surface.

4. Spread 1 teaspoon hoisin sauce in center of sheet; top with 2 to 3 shrimp, ¼ cup lettuce, about ¼ cup rice noodles, 1 teaspoon basil, and 1 teaspoon mint. Fold sides of sheet over filling, roll up jelly-roll fashion, and gently press seam to seal. Place roll, seam side down, on a serving platter; cover to keep from drying. Repeat procedure with remaining rice paper, hoisin sauce, shrimp, lettuce, rice noodles, basil, and mint.

5. To prepare dipping sauce, combine soy sauce and next 7 ingredients in a small bowl; stir with a whisk.

CALORIES 140; FAT 0.8g (sat 0.1g, mono 0.1g, poly 0.3g); PROTEIN 9g; CARB 23.5g; FIBER 0.7g; CHOL 47mg; IRON 1.3mg; SODIUM 385mg; CALC 32mg

Noodle-Vegetable Toss

Rice noodles make this a hearty dish that doesn't leave you feeling overly full.

Yield: 3 servings (serving size: 1⅓ cups)

6 cups water

6 ounces uncooked linguine-style rice noodles (such as Thai Kitchen)

1 tablespoon sugar

2 tablespoons water

1 tablespoon fish sauce

1 tablespoon fresh lime juice

2 cups packaged tricolor slaw mix

1 cup grated English cucumber

1 cup fresh bean sprouts

1 cup fresh cilantro leaves

½ cup chopped unsalted, dry-roasted peanuts

1. Bring 6 cups water to a boil in a large saucepan. Remove from heat; add rice noodles. Let soak 3 minutes or until tender. Drain.
2. While noodles soak, combine sugar and next 3 ingredients in a small bowl, stirring well with a whisk.
3. Combine noodles, slaw mix, and next 3 ingredients in a large bowl. Toss with sugar mixture. Sprinkle with peanuts. Serve immediately.

CALORIES 388; FAT 12g (sat 1.7g, mono 6g, poly 3.9g); PROTEIN 10.7g; CARB 61g; FIBER 3.8g; CHOL 0mg; IRON 2mg; SODIUM 397mg; CALC 49mg

INGREDIENT TIP

English, or seedless, cucumbers are usually twice the size of regular cucumbers and contain

fewer seeds and less water. They're also milder in flavor than regular cucumbers.

Shrimp Pad Thai

Pad Thai is the most popular noodle dish in Thailand. This supereasy recipe is a variation of Thai restaurant fare. Substitute 4 cups hot cooked linguine for the rice stick noodles if you have trouble finding them.

Yield: 6 servings (serving size: 1½ cups)

½ pound wide rice sticks (rice-flour noodles; banh poh)

¼ cup ketchup

2 tablespoons sugar

3 tablespoons fish sauce

½ teaspoon crushed red pepper

2 tablespoons vegetable oil, divided

1 pound medium shrimp, peeled and deveined

2 large eggs, lightly beaten

1 cup fresh bean sprouts

¾ cup (1-inch) sliced green onions

1 teaspoon bottled minced garlic

2 tablespoons chopped unsalted, dry-roasted peanuts

1. Place noodles in a large bowl. Add hot water to cover; let stand 12 minutes or until tender. Drain.

2. Combine ketchup, sugar, fish sauce, and pepper in a small bowl.

3. Heat 2 teaspoons oil in a large nonstick skillet over medium-high heat. Add shrimp; sauté 2 minutes or until shrimp reach desired degree of doneness. Remove shrimp from pan; keep warm.

4. Heat remaining 4 teaspoons oil in pan over medium-high heat. Add eggs; cook 30 seconds or until soft-scrambled, stirring constantly. Add sprouts, green onions, and garlic; cook 1 minute. Add noodles, ketchup mixture, and shrimp; cook 3 minutes or until heated. Sprinkle with peanuts.

CALORIES 343; FAT 9.2g (sat 1.6g, mono 2.6g, poly 3.9g); PROTEIN 21.3g; CARB 42.4g; FIBER 1.4g; CHOL 186mg; IRON 3mg; SODIUM 912mg; CALC 60mg

INGREDIENT TIP

Fish sauce is widely used in Southeast Asian cuisine as a condiment and flavoring. Combine it with sugar and lime juice to make a dipping sauce for vegetables and spring rolls, or use it as a base to add pungent flavor, as in this dish.

Singapore Mai Fun

Long popular in take-out menus, this curried noodle dish is a sure hit and ready in a snap—provided you have the ingredients prepped before you start. The leftovers are good cold, as well. You'll find skinny rice noodles in your supermarket's ethnic food section.

Yield: 6 servings (serving size: 1 cup)

1 (6-ounce) package skinny rice noodles (*py mai fun*)

½ cup fat-free, lower-sodium chicken broth

3 tablespoons lower-sodium soy sauce

1 teaspoon sugar

½ teaspoon salt

Cooking spray

1 tablespoon peanut oil, divided

1 large egg, lightly beaten

½ cup red bell pepper strips

1 tablespoon grated peeled fresh ginger

¼ teaspoon crushed red pepper

3 garlic cloves, minced

8 ounces skinless, boneless chicken breast, thinly sliced

1 tablespoon curry powder

8 ounces medium shrimp, peeled and deveined

1 cup (1-inch) sliced green onions

1. Cook rice noodles according to package directions, omitting salt and fat. Drain.

2. Combine broth, soy sauce, sugar, and salt; stir until sugar dissolves.

3. Heat a large nonstick skillet over medium-high heat; coat pan with cooking spray. Add 1 teaspoon oil. Add egg; stir-fry 30 seconds or until soft-scrambled, stirring constantly. Remove from pan. Wipe pan clean with a paper towel. Heat remaining 2 teaspoons oil in pan over medium-high heat. Add bell pepper strips, ginger, crushed red pepper, and garlic; stir-fry 15 seconds. Add chicken, and stir-fry 2 minutes. Add curry and shrimp; stir-fry 2 minutes. Stir in noodles, broth mixture, and egg; cook 1 minute or until thoroughly heated. Sprinkle with green onions.

CALORIES 237; FAT 4.6g (sat 1g, mono 1.7g, poly 1.3g); PROTEIN 19.7g; CARB 27.8g; FIBER 1.3g; CHOL 115mg; IRON 2.2mg; SODIUM 646mg; CALC 53mg

QUICK TIP

You can use a vegetable peeler or paring knife to peel fresh ginger, but a teaspoon also works well. Hold the ginger on a work surface, and move the tip of the spoon lengthwise across the ginger to scrape off the skin.

Peanut Chicken Soba Salad

You'll only need about 15 minutes to cook the chicken and noodles for this Asian salad. If you're short on time, substitute rotisserie chicken or leftover cooked chicken, and purchase preshredded carrots from your supermarket's produce section.

Yield: 4 servings (serving size: 1 cup salad and 1 teaspoon peanuts)

2 cups water

2 (6-ounce) skinless, boneless chicken breast halves

4 black peppercorns

1 bay leaf

2 tablespoons roasted peanut oil

1 tablespoon rice vinegar

2 teaspoons lower-sodium soy sauce

1 teaspoon honey

1 teaspoon chili garlic sauce (such as Lee Kum Kee)

½ teaspoon salt

2 cups cooked soba (about 4 ounces uncooked buckwheat noodles)

1 cup grated carrot

½ cup thinly sliced green onions

¼ cup minced red onion

¼ cup chopped fresh basil

4 teaspoons chopped unsalted, dry-roasted peanuts

Lime wedges (optional)

1. Combine first 4 ingredients in a medium saucepan; bring to a boil. Cover, remove from heat, and let stand 15 minutes or until chicken reaches desired degree of doneness. Remove chicken from pan, and discard peppercorns, bay leaf, and cooking liquid. Shred chicken; place in a large bowl.

2. Combine oil and next 5 ingredients, stirring with a whisk. Pour over chicken; let stand 5 minutes. Add soba noodles and next 4 ingredients to chicken mixture, and toss well. Sprinkle with peanuts. Garnish with lime wedges, if desired.

CALORIES 256; FAT 9.5g (sat 1.7g, mono 4.2g, poly 2.9g); PROTEIN 23.9g; CARB 19.5g; FIBER 2.5g; CHOL 49mg; IRON 1.3mg; SODIUM 538mg; CALC 30mg

Beef-Broccoli Lo Mein

Serve this quick-and-easy noodle dish with store-bought egg rolls and fortune cookies.

Yield: 6 servings (serving size: 1⅓ cups)

4 cups hot cooked spaghetti (about 8 ounces uncooked pasta)

1 teaspoon dark sesame oil

1 tablespoon peanut oil

1 tablespoon minced peeled fresh ginger

4 garlic cloves, minced

3 cups chopped broccoli

1½ cups vertically sliced onion

1 (1-pound) flank steak, trimmed and cut across grain into long, thin strips

3 tablespoons lower-sodium soy sauce

2 tablespoons brown sugar

1 tablespoon oyster sauce

1 tablespoon chile paste with garlic (such as sambal oelek)

1. Cook pasta according to package directions, omitting salt and fat; drain. Combine pasta and sesame oil, tossing well to coat.

2. While pasta cooks, heat peanut oil in a large nonstick skillet over medium-high heat. Add ginger and garlic; sauté 30 seconds. Add broccoli and onion; sauté 3 minutes. Add steak, and sauté 5 minutes or until desired degree of doneness. Add pasta mixture, soy sauce, and remaining ingredients; cook 1 minute or until lo mein is thoroughly heated, stirring constantly.

CALORIES 327; FAT 9.3g (sat 3g, mono 3.6g, poly 1.6g); PROTEIN 21.7g; CARB 39.1g; FIBER 2.9g; CHOL 36mg; IRON 3.6mg; SODIUM 382mg; CALC 47mg

QUICK TIP

For convenience, instead of buying broccoli and spending time cutting and separating the florets, purchase broccoli florets from your grocer's produce section.

all the
extras

Alfredo Sauce

Roman restaurateur Alfredo di Lello deserves credit for creating this luxurious dish in the 1920s by tossing hot, fresh egg noodles with melted butter and Parmigiano-Reggiano cheese. Along the way heavy cream was added to the sauce, and the dish evolved into an international favorite.

Yield: 6 servings (serving size: 1½ cups)

1 pound uncooked fettuccine

1 tablespoon butter

1¼ cups half-and-half

¾ cup (3 ounces) grated fresh Parmesan cheese

½ teaspoon salt

¼ teaspoon black pepper

1. Cook pasta according to package directions, omitting salt and fat.

2. Melt butter in a large skillet over medium heat. Add half-and-half, cheese, salt, and pepper; cook 1 minute, stirring constantly. Reduce heat; add pasta, tossing gently to coat.

CALORIES 427; FAT 14.6g (sat 7.8g, mono 4.2g, poly 1.3g); PROTEIN 17.2g; CARB 56.5g; FIBER 2.1g; CHOL 105mg; IRON 3.6mg; SODIUM 479mg; CALC 245mg

NUTRITION TIP

We used half-and-half instead of whipping cream and decreased the amount of butter and cheese ever so slightly to lower the fat by about 10 grams per serving.

Salsa Arrabbiata

A tomato-based pasta sauce, salsa arrabbiata—literally "angry sauce"—is made in countless versions in Italy, sometimes with meat, sometimes without, but always with some kind of hot pepper.

Yield: 6 servings (serving size: 1⅓ cups)

6 quarts water

2 teaspoons salt

1 pound uncooked campanelle pasta

1½ tablespoons olive oil

1½ cups (¼-inch-thick) onion wedges

3 bay leaves

1 (3-ounce) prosciutto end piece, cut into ½-inch pieces

½ cup pepperoncini peppers, drained, seeded, and thinly sliced

1 (28-ounce) can plum tomatoes, undrained and chopped

1 cup (4 ounces) grated fresh Parmigiano-Reggiano cheese

1. Bring 6 quarts water and 2 teaspoons salt to a boil in a large stockpot. Stir in campanelle pasta; partially cover, and return to a boil, stirring frequently. Cook 6 minutes or until pasta is almost al dente, stirring occasionally. Drain pasta in a colander over a bowl, reserving 1 cup cooking liquid.

2. While pasta cooks, heat oil in a Dutch oven over medium-high heat. Add onion, bay leaves, and prosciutto; sauté 5 minutes or until onion softens. Add peppers, and sauté 1 minute. Stir in reserved 1 cup cooking liquid and tomatoes; bring to a boil. Reduce heat, and simmer 10 minutes or until sauce thickens. Discard bay leaves.

3. Add pasta to Dutch oven; cook 1 minute, stirring well to coat, or until pasta is al dente. Remove from heat; stir in cheese.

CALORIES 331; FAT 7.7g (sat 2.7g, mono 2.8g, poly 0.8g); PROTEIN 15.1g; CARB 50.6g; FIBER 2g; CHOL 18mg; IRON 2.6mg; SODIUM 965mg; CALC 182mg

FLAVOR TIP

The spicy heat comes from small, whole, pickled peppers that are labeled pepperoncini or pepperoncino. Although these are milder than pickled cherry peppers, they provide plenty of spice.

Clam Sauce

While some clam sauces call for anchovies or a hot red chile, ours relies on tomatoes and basil for flavor.

Yield: 4 servings (serving size: 1 cup)

3 (6½-ounce) cans minced clams, undrained

1 tablespoon olive oil

2 garlic cloves, minced

1⅓ cups chopped tomato

2 tablespoons minced fresh parsley

1 teaspoon crushed red pepper

½ cup dry white wine

4 cups hot cooked fettuccine (about 8 ounces uncooked pasta)

2 tablespoons chopped fresh basil

1. Drain clams in a colander over a bowl, reserving liquid.
2. Heat oil in a large nonstick skillet over medium heat. Add garlic; cook 30 seconds, stirring constantly. Add tomato, parsley, and pepper; cook 1 minute. Add wine; cook 30 seconds. Add reserved clam liquid and pasta, tossing to coat; cook 3 minutes or until liquid almost evaporates, stirring frequently. Stir in clams and basil. Serve immediately.

CALORIES 289; FAT 6.3g (sat 1.1g, mono 3.3g, poly 1.1g); PROTEIN 9.8g; CARB 48.5g; FIBER 2.8g; CHOL 64mg; IRON 3.7mg; SODIUM 316mg; CALC 49mg

Basic Marinara

Rely on a large Dutch oven or stockpot because this recipe makes enough sauce for several meals. Cook at a low simmer—just a few bubbles every few seconds will yield the deepest taste.

Yield: about 12 cups (serving size: ½ cup)

3 tablespoons olive oil

3 cups chopped yellow onion (about 3 medium)

1 tablespoon sugar

3 tablespoons minced garlic (about 6 cloves)

2 teaspoons salt

2 teaspoons dried basil

1½ teaspoons dried oregano

1 teaspoon dried thyme

1 teaspoon freshly ground black pepper

½ teaspoon fennel seeds, crushed

2 tablespoons balsamic vinegar

2 cups fat-free, lower-sodium chicken broth

3 (28-ounce) cans no-salt-added crushed tomatoes, undrained

1. Heat oil in a large Dutch oven over medium heat. Add onion to pan; cook 4 minutes, stirring frequently. Add sugar and next 7 ingredients; cook 1 minute, stirring constantly. Stir in vinegar; cook 30 seconds. Add broth and tomatoes; bring to a simmer. Cook over low heat 55 minutes or until sauce thickens, stirring occasionally.

CALORIES 50; FAT 1.8g (sat 0.2g, mono 1.3g, poly 0.2g); PROTEIN 1.3g; CARB 8g; FIBER 2.1g; CHOL 0mg; IRON 0.5mg; SODIUM 270mg; CALC 28mg

FREEZER TIP

Ladle room-temperature or chilled sauce into plastic containers or zip-top plastic freezer bags. Seal and freeze for up to four months. Consider freezing the sauce in 1-cup increments (two servings' worth). That way, you can pull out exactly as much as you want for future meals.

Mushroom Sauce

Because fresh porcini mushrooms are hard to come by in this country, we've combined dried porcini with fresh cremini (baby portobellos) to create this flavorful sauce.

Yield: 4 servings (serving size: about 1½ cups)

1½ cups dried porcini mushrooms (about 1½ ounces)

2 teaspoons olive oil

½ cup finely chopped prosciutto (about 2 ounces)

½ cup finely chopped onion

4 cups sliced cremini or button mushrooms (about 8 ounces)

½ teaspoon grated lemon rind

½ teaspoon salt

¼ teaspoon black pepper

2 garlic cloves, minced

1 cup fat-free, lower-sodium chicken broth

¾ cup dry red wine

1 tablespoon cornstarch

1 tablespoon water

4 cups hot cooked cavatappi (about 2 cups uncooked pasta)

1. Combine boiling water and porcini mushrooms in a bowl; cover and let stand 30 minutes. Drain. Rinse and coarsely chop porcini mushrooms.

2. Heat oil in a medium skillet over medium-high heat. Add prosciutto, and sauté 1 minute. Add onion; sauté 3 minutes or until tender. Stir in porcini mushrooms, cremini mushrooms, and next 4 ingredients; cook 4 minutes or until browned, stirring frequently. Stir in broth and wine, scraping pan to loosen browned bits. Bring to a boil; cook 3 minutes. Combine cornstarch and 1 tablespoon water in a small bowl. Add cornstarch mixture to pan; bring to a boil. Cook 1 minute, stirring constantly. Add pasta, tossing to coat.

CALORIES 304; FAT 5.1g (sat 1g, mono 2.6g, poly 1g); PROTEIN 15.4g; CARB 48.9g; FIBER 4.6g; CHOL 8mg; IRON 4.9mg; SODIUM 627mg; CALC 24mg

INGREDIENT TIP

Also known as boletes, cèpes, or steinpilz, porcini mushrooms are most often found

dried in the United States. If you find fresh porcinis, choose those that are pale to tan in color, and avoid those that crumble easily.

Pesto

We reduced the amount of oil, pine nuts, cheese, and butter usually found in a classic pesto, cutting 28 grams of fat per serving without losing any flavor. Avoid packing the basil leaves when you measure them so you won't use too much.

Yield: 4 servings (serving size: about 1 cup pasta)

4 cups fresh basil leaves

2 tablespoons pine nuts

2 tablespoons extra-virgin olive oil

¼ teaspoon salt

2 garlic cloves, peeled

½ cup (2 ounces) grated fresh Parmesan cheese

2 tablespoons grated fresh Romano cheese

2 teaspoons butter, softened

2 cups uncooked penne (about 8 ounces)

1. Combine first 5 ingredients in a food processor; process until finely minced. Place in a large bowl. Stir in cheeses and butter until blended.

2. Cook pasta according to package directions, omitting salt and fat. Drain in a colander over a bowl, reserving 3 tablespoons cooking liquid. Add pasta and reserved cooking liquid to pesto, tossing to coat.

CALORIES 390; FAT 17g (sat 5.4g, mono 6.5g, poly 2.1g); PROTEIN 14.5g; CARB 45.3g; FIBER 3.2g; CHOL 18mg; IRON 4mg; SODIUM 352mg; CALC 281mg

Sage, Bay, and Garlic Dipping Oil

Bay and sage permeate this garlicky oil, infusing it with wonderful earthy, woodsy flavors. Serve this oil, or the others below, with Ciabatta (recipe on page 247), a purchased focaccia, or a loaf of Italian bread. Pour the oil into small, wide bowls to facilitate dipping, and garnish each oil with its seasonings. Refrigerate oils up to a week in glass containers. Toss leftover oil with pasta, or use it in salad dressing.

Yield: 12 servings (serving size: 2 teaspoons)

½ cup olive oil

2 garlic cloves, crushed

2 fresh sage leaves

1 bay leaf

1. Combine all ingredients in a small, heavy saucepan. Cook over medium-low heat until thermometer registers 180°. Reduce heat to low, and cook 20 minutes (do not allow temperature to rise above 200°). Cool to room temperature. Drain oil mixture through a sieve into a bowl, and discard solids.

CALORIES 80; FAT 9g (sat 1.2g, mono 6.6g, poly 0.8g); PROTEIN 0g; CARB 0g; FIBER 0g; CHOL 0mg; IRON 0mg; SODIUM 0mg; CALC 0mg

Basil Dipping Oil

Yield: 12 servings (serving size: 2 teaspoons)

2 cups chopped fresh basil leaves (about 2 [¾-ounce] packages)

½ cup olive oil

1. Combine basil and oil in a small, heavy saucepan. Cook over medium-low heat until thermometer registers 180°. Reduce heat to low; cook 20 minutes (do not allow temperature to rise above 200°). Cool to room temperature. Drain oil mixture through a sieve into a bowl; discard solids.

CALORIES 80; FAT 9g (sat 1.2g, mono 6.6g, poly 0.8g); PROTEIN 0g; CARB 0g; FIBER 0g; CHOL 0mg; IRON 0mg; SODIUM 0mg; CALC 0mg

Three-Pepper Dipping Oil

Yield: 12 servings (serving size: 2 teaspoons)

½ cup olive oil

1 pepperoncini pepper, halved lengthwise

1 whole dried hot red chile, crushed

2 whole black peppercorns

1. Combine all ingredients in a small, heavy saucepan. Cook mixture over medium-low heat until thermometer registers 180°. Reduce heat to low, and cook 20 minutes (do not allow temperature to rise above 200°). Cool mixture to room temperature. Drain oil mixture through a sieve into a bowl, and discard solids.

CALORIES 80; FAT 9g (sat 1.2g, mono 6.6g, poly 0.8g); PROTEIN 0g; CARB 0g; FIBER 0g; CHOL 0mg; IRON 0mg; SODIUM 0mg; CALC 0mg

Ciabatta

This bread gets its name from its shape; ciabatta is Italian for "slipper." Letting the sponge rest for 12 hours develops complex yeast flavor, a soft interior, and a crisp, thin crust.

Yield: 2 loaves, 16 servings (serving size: 1 slice)

Sponge:

4.75 ounces bread flour (about 1 cup)

½ cup warm fat-free milk (100° to 110°)

¼ cup warm water (100° to 110°)

1 tablespoon honey

1 package dry yeast (about 2¼ teaspoons)

Dough:

16.63 ounces bread flour, divided (about 3½ cups)

½ cup semolina or pasta flour

¾ cup warm water (100° to 110°)

½ cup warm fat-free milk (100° to 110°)

1½ teaspoons salt

1 package dry yeast (about 2¼ teaspoons)

3 tablespoons semolina or pasta flour, divided

1. To prepare sponge, weigh or lightly spoon 1 cup flour into a dry measuring cup; level with a knife. Combine 1 cup flour and next 4 ingredients in a large bowl, stirring well with a whisk. Cover; chill 12 hours.

2. To prepare dough, let sponge stand at room temperature 30 minutes. Weigh or lightly spoon 3½ cups bread flour and ½ cup semolina flour into dry measuring cups, and level with a knife. Add 3 cups bread flour, ½ cup semolina flour, ¾ cup warm water, ½ cup warm milk, salt, and 1 package yeast to sponge, and stir well to form a soft dough. Turn dough out onto a floured surface. Knead until smooth and elastic (about 8 minutes), and add enough of remaining bread flour, 1 tablespoon at a time, to prevent dough from sticking to hands. Divide dough in half.

3. Working with 1 portion at a time (cover remaining dough to prevent drying), roll each into a 13 x 5–inch oval. Place, 3 inches apart, on a large baking sheet sprinkled with 2 tablespoons semolina flour. Taper ends of dough to form a "slipper." Sprinkle 1 tablespoon semolina flour over dough. Cover and let rise in a warm place (85°), free from drafts, 45 minutes or until doubled in size. (Gently press two fingers into dough. If indentation remains, dough has risen enough.)

4. Preheat oven to 425°.

5. Uncover dough. Bake at 425° for 18 minutes or until the loaves are lightly browned and sound hollow when tapped. Remove from pan, and cool on a wire rack.

CALORIES 150; FAT 0.1g (sat 0g, mono 0.1g, poly 0g); PROTEIN 6.3g; CARB 32.1g; FIBER 1.3g; CHOL 0mg; IRON 2.1mg; SODIUM 227mg; CALC 21mg

Garlic-Thyme Focaccia

Two kinds of salt add flavor and crunch. For a spicy variation, infuse the oil with 1/2 teaspoon crushed red pepper along with the garlic; strain through a sieve before brushing the flavored oil onto the dough.

Yield: 10 servings (serving size: 1 piece)

1 teaspoon sugar

1 package dry yeast (about 2¼ teaspoons)

1 cup warm water (100° to 110°)

½ teaspoon fine sea salt

11.25 ounces all-purpose flour, divided (about 2⅓ cups plus 2 tablespoons)

Cooking spray

1 tablespoon olive oil

2 garlic cloves, thinly sliced

1 tablespoon chopped fresh thyme

¾ teaspoon coarse sea salt

Thyme sprigs (optional)

1. Dissolve sugar and yeast in 1 cup warm water in a large bowl; let stand 5 minutes. Stir in fine sea salt. Weigh or lightly spoon flour into dry measuring cups and spoons; level with a knife. Add 2 cups plus 2 tablespoons flour, stirring to form a soft dough. Turn dough out onto a floured surface. Knead dough until smooth and elastic (about 8 minutes); add enough of remaining ⅓ cup flour, 1 tablespoon at a time, to prevent dough from sticking to hands.

2. Place dough in a large bowl coated with cooking spray, turning to coat top. Cover and let rise in a warm place (85°), free from drafts, 45 minutes or until doubled in size. (Gently press two fingers into dough. If indentation remains, dough has risen enough.)

3. Heat oil in a small skillet over medium-low heat. Add garlic; cook 5 minutes or until fragrant. Remove garlic from oil with a slotted spoon; discard garlic, and remove pan from heat.

4. Place dough on a baking sheet coated with cooking spray; pat into a 12 x 8–inch rectangle. Brush garlic oil over dough; sprinkle with thyme. Cover and let rise 25 minutes or until doubled in size.

5. Preheat oven to 425°.

6. Make indentations in top of dough using the handle of a wooden spoon or your fingertips; sprinkle dough evenly with coarse sea salt. Bake at 425° for 14 minutes or until lightly browned. Remove from pan; cool on a wire rack. Garnish with thyme sprigs.

CALORIES 128; FAT 1.7g (sat 0.2g, mono 1g, poly 0.3g); PROTEIN 3.5g; CARB 24.2g; FIBER 1.1g; CHOL 0mg; IRON 1.6mg; SODIUM 289mg; CALC 7mg

INGREDIENT TIP

Thyme comes in dozens of varieties, but most cooks use French thyme. Because the leaves are so small, they often don't require chopping, but you'll want to chop them for this recipe.

Bruschetta

Broil the bread slices for two minutes on each side instead of grilling them, if desired.

Yield: 8 appetizers (serving size: 1 appetizer)

8 (¾-inch-thick) diagonally cut Italian bread slices (about 8 ounces)

Cooking spray

1 garlic clove, halved

4 teaspoons extra-virgin olive oil

¼ teaspoon kosher salt

Parsley sprigs (optional)

1. Preheat grill. Place bread slices on grill rack coated with cooking spray, and cook 2 minutes on each side or until lightly browned. Remove from grill.

2. Rub cut sides of garlic over 1 side of each bread slice, and brush with oil; sprinkle with salt. Garnish with parsley sprigs, if desired.

CALORIES 99; FAT 2.6g (sat 0.3g, mono 1.7g, poly 0.2g); PROTEIN 2.6g; CARB 16.1g; FIBER 0.8g; CHOL 0mg; IRON 0.6mg; SODIUM 203mg; CALC 6mg

Spicy Peppercorn and Pecorino Breadsticks

With black and red pepper, these breadsticks pack some heat. If you don't have semolina, you can use cornmeal.

Yield: 24 servings (serving size: 1 breadstick)

1 package dry yeast (about 2¼ teaspoons)

1⅓ cups warm water (100° to 110°)

16.63 ounces bread flour, divided (about 3½ cups)

2 tablespoons extra-virgin olive oil

2 teaspoons coarsely ground black pepper

1¾ teaspoons salt

¾ teaspoon crushed red pepper

1 cup (4 ounces) grated fresh pecorino Romano cheese

Cooking spray

2 tablespoons ground semolina

1. Dissolve yeast in 1⅓ cups warm water in a large bowl; let stand 5 minutes. Weigh or lightly spoon flour into dry measuring cups; level with a knife. Add ½ cup flour to yeast mixture, stirring with a whisk. Let stand 30 minutes. Add remaining 3 cups flour, olive oil, black pepper, salt, and red pepper; stir until a soft dough forms. Turn dough out onto a lightly floured surface. Knead until smooth and elastic (about 8 minutes); cover and let rest 10 minutes.

2. Knead in half of cheese; cover and let rest 5 minutes. Knead in remaining cheese.

3. Place dough in a large bowl coated with cooking spray, turning to coat top. Cover and let rise in a warm place (85°), free from drafts, 45 minutes or until doubled in size. (Gently press two fingers into dough. If indentation remains, dough has risen enough.) Punch dough down. Roll dough into a 12 x 8–inch rectangle on a lightly floured surface.

4. Preheat oven to 450°.

5. Sprinkle 1 tablespoon semolina onto each of 2 baking sheets. Cut dough in half lengthwise to form 2 (12 x 4–inch) rectangles. Cut each rectangle crosswise into 12 (1-inch-wide) strips. Working with 1 strip at a time (cover remaining dough to prevent drying), gently roll each strip into a 15-inch-long rope. Place rope on prepared pan, and repeat procedure with remaining strips, placing 12 on each pan. Cover and let dough rise 20 minutes.

6. Uncover dough; bake each pan at 450° for 12 minutes. Remove breadsticks from pans; cool completely on wire racks.

CALORIES 99; FAT 2.4g (sat 1g, mono 1.2g, poly 0.1g); PROTEIN 4.4g; CARB 15.7g; FIBER 0.7g; CHOL 5mg; IRON 1.1mg; SODIUM 228mg; CALC 52mg

Parmesan and Cracked Pepper Grissini

Yield: 12 servings (serving size: 2 breadsticks)

1 package dry yeast (about 2¼ teaspoons)

1 cup warm water (100° to 110°)

14.25 ounces bread flour, divided (about 3 cups)

1¼ teaspoons salt

Cooking spray

1 teaspoon water

1 large egg white, lightly beaten

½ cup (2 ounces) grated fresh Parmesan cheese

1 tablespoon cracked black pepper

2 teaspoons cornmeal, divided

1. Dissolve yeast in 1 cup warm water in a large bowl; let stand 5 minutes.

2. Weigh or lightly spoon flour into dry measuring cups; level with a knife. Add 2¾ cups flour and salt to yeast mixture; stir until a soft dough forms. Turn dough out onto a floured surface. Knead until smooth and elastic (about 8 minutes); add enough of remaining flour, 1 tablespoon at a time, to prevent dough from sticking to hands (dough will feel tacky).

3. Place dough in a large bowl coated with cooking spray, turning to coat top. Cover and let rise in a warm place (85°), free from drafts, 45 minutes or until doubled in size. (Gently press two fingers into dough. If indentation remains, dough has risen enough.)

4. Punch dough down. Cover and let rest 5 minutes. Turn dough out onto a lightly floured surface; roll into a 12 x 8–inch rectangle.

5. Combine 1 teaspoon water and egg white, stirring with a whisk; brush evenly over dough. Sprinkle dough with cheese and pepper. Lightly coat dough with cooking spray; cover with plastic wrap. Gently press toppings into dough; remove plastic wrap.

6. Sprinkle each of 2 baking sheets with 1 teaspoon cornmeal. Cut dough in half lengthwise to form 2 (12 x 4–inch) rectangles. Cut each rectangle crosswise into 12 (1-inch) strips.

7. Working with 1 strip at a time (cover remaining strips to prevent drying), gently roll each strip into a log. Holding ends of log between forefinger and thumb of each hand, gently pull log into a 14-inch rope, slightly shaking it up and down while pulling. (You can also roll each strip into a 14-inch rope on a lightly floured surface.) Place rope on a prepared pan, curving into a series of shapes so that rope fits on pan.

8. Repeat procedure with remaining strips, placing 12 on each pan. Lightly coat ropes with cooking spray. Cover and let rise 20 minutes or until doubled in size.

9. Preheat oven to 450°.

10. Uncover dough; bake at 450° for 6 minutes with 1 pan on bottom rack and 1 pan on second rack from top. Rotate pans; bake an additional 6 minutes or until golden brown.

11. Remove breadsticks from pans; cool completely on wire racks.

CALORIES 148; FAT 1.9g (sat 0.9g, mono 0.4g, poly 0.3g); PROTEIN 6.4g; CARB 25.9g; FIBER 1.1g; CHOL 3mg; IRON 1.8mg; SODIUM 326mg; CALC 64mg

Figs and Prosciutto with Mint and Shaved Parmigiano-Reggiano

Ripe figs are the secret to this simple yet refined salad. It's best made just before serving.

Yield: 8 servings (serving size: 4 fig quarters, about ½ ounce prosciutto, and ⅛ ounce cheese)

8 fresh figs, quartered

2 teaspoons extra-virgin olive oil

¼ teaspoon cracked black pepper

1 ounce Parmigiano-Reggiano cheese, thinly shaved

12 mint leaves, thinly sliced

4 ounces thinly sliced prosciutto

1. Place figs in a bowl; drizzle with oil. Sprinkle figs with pepper; toss gently.

2. Place fig mixture in center of a platter; top with cheese and mint. Top with prosciutto.

CALORIES 90; FAT 3.4g (sat 1.2g, mono 1.8g, poly 0.3g); PROTEIN 4.8g; CARB 9.5g; FIBER 1.4g; CHOL 11mg; IRON 0.3mg; SODIUM 270mg; CALC 64mg

NUTRITION TIP

The dense texture and subtle, sweet flavor of fresh figs are hard to beat. Figs are a good source of fiber, manganese, potassium, and vitamin B$_6$.

Orange, Arugula, and Kalamata Olive Salad

Blood oranges add vibrant red color, so use them if you can find them. Pit the olives by crushing them with the blade of a chef's knife.

Yield: 8 servings (serving size: about 1¼ cups)

2 tablespoons fresh lemon juice

1½ teaspoons extra-virgin olive oil

½ teaspoon salt

⅛ teaspoon freshly ground black pepper

8 cups trimmed arugula (about 8 ounces)

2 cups thinly sliced fennel bulb

¾ cup vertically sliced red onion

12 sliced pitted kalamata olives

2 cups coarsely chopped orange sections (about 2 pounds)

1. Combine first 4 ingredients. Combine arugula, fennel, onion, and olives in a large bowl. Drizzle lemon mixture over arugula mixture; toss gently to coat. Top with orange sections.

CALORIES 62; FAT 2.6g (sat 0.3g, mono 1.8g, poly 0.3g); PROTEIN 1.4g; CARB 9.4g; FIBER 2.3g; CHOL 0mg; IRON 0.6mg; SODIUM 254mg; CALC 65mg

Pesto Caesar Salad

Forget bottled dressings—this homemade Caesar dressing makes this salad simply divine. Serve as a side to any traditional pasta main dish, or make it a meal all its own by tossing in some grilled chicken.

Yield: 6 servings

3 ounces French bread baguette, cut into ½-inch cubes

1½ teaspoons extra-virgin olive oil

Cooking spray

2 ounces Parmigiano-Reggiano cheese

¼ cup organic canola mayonnaise (such as Spectrum)

3 tablespoons refrigerated pesto

4 teaspoons water

2 teaspoons fresh lemon juice

1 teaspoon anchovy paste

½ teaspoon Worcestershire sauce

½ teaspoon Dijon mustard

⅛ teaspoon hot pepper sauce (such as Tabasco)

1 garlic clove, minced

12 cups torn romaine lettuce

1. Preheat oven to 400°.

2. Place bread in a large bowl; drizzle with oil. Toss to coat. Arrange bread in a single layer on a baking sheet coated with cooking spray. Bake at 400° for 10 minutes or until golden, turning once.

3. Grate 2 tablespoons cheese; shave remaining cheese to equal about 6 tablespoons. Set shaved cheese aside.

4. Combine grated cheese, mayonnaise, and next 8 ingredients in a medium bowl, stirring well with a whisk. Combine croutons and lettuce in a large bowl. Drizzle mayonnaise mixture over lettuce mixture; toss to coat.

5. Place 1⅓ cups salad on each of 6 plates; top each serving with 1 tablespoon shaved cheese.

CALORIES 202; FAT 14.3g (sat 2.3g, mono 6.2g, poly 5.4g); PROTEIN 6.2g; CARB 13.6g; FIBER 2.9g; CHOL 15mg; IRON 1.9mg; SODIUM 331mg; CALC 131mg

Sherried Zabaglione with Berries

Serve this light custard sauce immediately to enjoy its frothy texture. A double boiler cooks the delicate custard gently and eliminates the chance of curdling. The water that heats the custard must simmer, not boil. Regulate the water before placing the custard on top, and be conservative; once the top is in place, the water tends to heat up. Any berries will work with this tasty sauce.

Yield: 4 servings (serving size: ½ cup berries and about ¼ cup zabaglione)

5 tablespoons sugar

3 tablespoons cream sherry

2 large eggs

3 tablespoons reduced-fat sour cream

2 cups fresh blackberries

Mint sprigs (optional)

1. Combine first 3 ingredients in top of a double boiler. Cook over simmering water until thick (about 4 minutes) and a thermometer registers 160°, stirring mixture constantly with a whisk. Remove top pan from heat; whisk the mixture an additional 2 minutes. Gently whisk in sour cream. Serve zabaglione immediately over berries. Garnish with mint sprigs, if desired.

CALORIES 157; FAT 4.2g (sat 1.7g, mono 1.4g, poly 0.6g); PROTEIN 4.2g; CARB 25.9g; FIBER 3.8g; CHOL 112mg; IRON 0.8mg; SODIUM 39mg; CALC 55mg

Tuscan Almond Biscotti

These crunchy, light cookies are a specialty of Prato, a city in Tuscany, where they are called cantucci. The biscotti will keep in airtight tins for up to a week.

Yield: 2 dozen (serving size: 1 biscotto)

7.9 ounces all-purpose flour (about 1¾ cups)

1 cup sugar

1 teaspoon baking powder

¼ teaspoon salt

1 cup whole almonds, toasted

2 large eggs

½ teaspoon almond extract

Cooking spray

1. Preheat oven to 375°.

2. Weigh or lightly spoon flour into dry measuring cups; level with a knife. Combine flour, sugar, baking powder, and salt in a large bowl. Place almonds in a food processor; pulse 10 times. Stir nuts into flour mixture.

3. Combine eggs and extract, stirring well with a whisk. Add egg mixture to flour mixture, stirring just until blended (dough will be crumbly). Turn dough out onto a lightly floured surface; knead lightly 7 or 8 times. Divide dough into 2 equal portions. Shape each portion into a 6-inch-long roll. Place rolls 6 inches apart on a baking sheet coated with cooking spray, and pat to 1-inch thickness. Bake at 375° for 25 minutes or until lightly browned. Cool 5 minutes on a wire rack.

4. Cut each roll crosswise into 12 (½-inch) slices. Stand slices upright on baking sheet.

5. Bake 14 minutes (cookies will be slightly soft in center but will harden as they cool). Remove from baking sheet, and cool completely on wire rack.

CALORIES 102; FAT 3.4g (sat 0.4g, mono 2.1g, poly 0.8g); PROTEIN 2.7g; CARB 15.7g; FIBER 0.9g; CHOL 18mg; IRON 0.8mg; SODIUM 51mg; CALC 28mg

WINE TIP

In Italy, this type of biscotti is typically served at the end of a meal with a glass of vin santo, a sweet dessert wine.

Strawberries with Crunchy Almond Topping

This easy but stylish dessert is best made early in the day to let the strawberries macerate in the sweetened almond liqueur.

Yield: 6 servings (serving size: ½ cup strawberries, 1 crushed cookie, and 1 tablespoon sour cream)

6 cups sliced strawberries

½ cup sugar

2 tablespoons amaretto (almond-flavored liqueur)

6 amaretti cookies, crushed

6 tablespoons reduced-fat sour cream

1. Combine first 3 ingredients in a bowl. Cover and chill 4 to 8 hours. Spoon into individual dessert dishes. Sprinkle with crushed cookies; top with sour cream.

CALORIES 207; FAT 2.6g (sat 0.4g, mono 0.3g, poly 0.3g); PROTEIN 2.8g; CARB 44g; FIBER 4.8g; CHOL 2mg; IRON 0.7mg; SODIUM 29mg; CALC 32mg

Honey Gelato

Store the gelato in an airtight container in the freezer for up to one week; it won't freeze solid but will maintain a soft texture. Purchased rolled wafer cookies make a delicate accompaniment to this rich dessert.

Yield: 8 servings (serving size: ½ cup)

½ cup honey

⅓ cup nonfat dry milk

1 (12-ounce) can evaporated fat-free milk

⅛ teaspoon salt

4 large egg yolks

1 cup 2% reduced-fat milk

Mint sprigs (optional)

1. Combine first 3 ingredients in a medium, heavy saucepan. Heat mixture over medium heat until honey dissolves, stirring frequently (do not boil). Remove from heat.

2. Combine salt and egg yolks in a large bowl, stirring with a whisk. Gradually add honey mixture to egg mixture, stirring constantly with a whisk. Place honey mixture in pan; cook over medium heat until mixture reaches 180° (about 3 minutes), stirring constantly (do not boil). Remove from heat; stir in reduced-fat milk. Cool completely.

3. Pour mixture into freezer can of an ice-cream freezer; freeze according to manufacturer's instructions. Spoon gelato into a freezer-safe container. Cover and freeze 2 hours or until firm. Garnish with mint sprigs, if desired.

CALORIES 153; FAT 3.3g (sat 1.2g, mono 1.2g, poly 0.4g); PROTEIN 6.7g; CARB 25.4g; FIBER 0g; CHOL 111mg; IRON 0.5mg; SODIUM 121mg; CALC 208mg

INGREDIENT TIP

Honey is a good choice for gelato because its resistance to freezing ensures creaminess. We like mild clover and lavender honeys in this recipe.

Tiramisu

Place toothpicks in the center and in each corner of the dish to prevent the plastic wrap from sticking to the tiramisu as it chills.

Yield: 8 servings

Espresso Drizzle:

½ cup water

2 tablespoons granulated sugar

2 tablespoons instant espresso granules

2 tablespoons Kahlúa (coffee-flavored liqueur)

Filling:

1 (8-ounce) block fat-free cream cheese, softened

1 (3.5-ounce) carton mascarpone cheese

⅓ cup granulated sugar

¼ cup packed brown sugar

2 tablespoons Kahlúa

Remaining Ingredients:

24 cakelike ladyfingers (2 [3-ounce] packages)

1½ teaspoons unsweetened cocoa

½ ounce bittersweet chocolate, grated

Chocolate curls (optional)

1. To prepare espresso drizzle, combine first 3 ingredients in a small saucepan over medium-high heat; bring to a boil. Cook 1 minute, stirring occasionally. Remove from heat; stir in 2 tablespoons liqueur. Cool completely.

2. To prepare filling, combine cheeses in a large bowl, and beat with a mixer at medium speed until smooth. Add ⅓ cup granulated sugar, brown sugar, and 2 tablespoons liqueur; beat at medium speed until well blended.

3. Split ladyfingers in half lengthwise. Arrange 24 ladyfinger halves, cut sides up, in bottom of an 8-inch square baking dish. Drizzle half of espresso drizzle over ladyfinger halves. Spread half of filling over ladyfinger halves, and repeat procedure with remaining ladyfinger halves, espresso drizzle, and filling. Combine 1½ teaspoons cocoa and chocolate; sprinkle evenly over top of filling. Cover and chill 2 hours. Garnish with chocolate curls, if desired.

CALORIES 260; FAT 8g (sat 4.1g, mono 2.2g, poly 0.5g); PROTEIN 7.1g; CARB 38.4g; FIBER 0.5g; CHOL 55mg; IRON 0.8mg; SODIUM 317mg; CALC 104mg

INGREDIENT TIP

Find ladyfingers in the bakery section of your supermarket. Most come already split in half

lengthwise, but you can split them yourself with a serrated knife, if needed.

Nutritional Analysis

How to Use It and Why

Glance at the end of any *Cooking Light* recipe, and you'll see how committed we are to helping you make the best of today's light cooking. With chefs, registered dietitians, home economists, and a computer system that analyzes every ingredient we use, *Cooking Light* gives you authoritative dietary detail like no other magazine. We go to such lengths so you can see how our recipes fit into your healthful eating plan. If you're trying to lose weight, the calorie and fat figures will probably help most. But if you're keeping a close eye on the sodium, cholesterol, and saturated fat in your diet, we provide those numbers, too. And because many women don't get enough iron or calcium, we can help there, as well. Finally, there's a fiber analysis for those of us who don't get enough roughage.

Here's a helpful guide to put our nutritional analysis numbers into perspective. Remember, one size doesn't fit all, so take your lifestyle, age, and circumstances into consideration when determining your nutrition needs. For example, pregnant or breast-feeding women need more protein, calories, and calcium. And women older than 50 need 1,200mg of calcium daily, 200mg more than the amount recommended for younger women.

In Our Nutritional Analysis, We Use These Abbreviations

sat	saturated fat	**CHOL**	cholesterol
mono	monounsaturated fat	**CALC**	calcium
poly	polyunsaturated fat	**g**	gram
CARB	carbohydrates	**mg**	milligram

Daily Nutrition Guide

	Women ages 25 to 50	Women over 50	Men over 24
Calories	2,000	2,000 or less	2,700
Protein	50g	50g or less	63g
Fat	65g or less	65g or less	88g or less
Saturated Fat	20g or less	20g or less	27g or less
Carbohydrates	304g	304g	410g
Fiber	25g to 35g	25g to 35g	25g to 35g
Cholesterol	300mg or less	300mg or less	300mg or less
Iron	18mg	8mg	8mg
Sodium	2,300mg or less	1,500mg or less	2,300mg or less
Calcium	1,000mg	1,200mg	1,000mg

The nutritional values used in our calculations either come from The Food Processor, Version 8.9 (ESHA Research), or are provided by food manufacturers.

Metric Equivalents

The information in the following charts is provided to help cooks outside the United States successfully use the recipes in this book. All equivalents are approximate.

Cooking/Oven Temperatures

	Fahrenheit	Celsius	Gas Mark
Freeze Water	32° F	0° C	
Room Temp.	68° F	20° C	
Boil Water	212° F	100° C	
Bake	325° F	160° C	3
	350° F	180° C	4
	375° F	190° C	5
	400° F	200° C	6
	425° F	220° C	7
	450° F	230° C	8
Broil			Grill

Liquid Ingredients by Volume

¼ tsp	=					1 ml		
½ tsp	=					2 ml		
1 tsp	=					5 ml		
3 tsp	=	1 tbl	=	½ fl oz	=	15 ml		
2 tbls	=	⅛ cup	=	1 fl oz	=	30 ml		
4 tbls	=	¼ cup	=	2 fl oz	=	60 ml		
5⅓ tbls	=	⅓ cup	=	3 fl oz	–	80 ml		
8 tbls	=	½ cup	=	4 fl oz	=	120 ml		
10⅔ tbls	=	⅔ cup	=	5 fl oz	=	160 ml		
12 tbls	–	¾ cup	=	6 fl oz	=	180 ml		
16 tbls	=	1 cup	=	8 fl oz	=	240 ml		
1 pt	=	2 cups	=	16 fl oz	=	480 ml		
1 qt	=	4 cups	=	32 fl oz	=	960 ml		
				33 fl oz	=	1000 ml	=	1 l

Dry Ingredients by Weight

(To convert ounces to grams, multiply the number of ounces by 30.)

1 oz	=	¹⁄₁₆ lb	=	30 g
4 oz	=	¼ lb	=	120 g
8 oz	=	½ lb	=	240 g
12 oz	=	¾ lb	=	360 g
16 oz	=	1 lb	=	480 g

Length

(To convert inches to centimeters, multiply the number of inches by 2.5.)

1 in	=			2.5 cm	
6 in	=	½ ft	=	15 cm	
12 in	=	1 ft	=	30 cm	
36 in	=	3 ft	= 1 yd =	90 cm	
40 in	=			100 cm	= 1 m

Equivalents for Different Types of Ingredients

Standard Cup	Fine Powder (ex. flour)	Grain (ex. rice)	Granular (ex. sugar)	Liquid Solids (ex. butter)	Liquid (ex. milk)
1	140 g	150 g	190 g	200 g	240 ml
¾	105 g	113 g	143 g	150 g	180 ml
⅔	93 g	100 g	125 g	133 g	160 ml
½	70 g	75 g	95 g	100 g	120 ml
⅓	47 g	50 g	63 g	67 g	80 ml
¼	35 g	38 g	48 g	50 g	60 ml
⅛	18 g	19 g	24 g	25 g	30 ml

Index